Joe Bonamassa

An Inside Look at the Guitar Style of Joe Bonamassa

by Toby Wine

Cover photo by Christie Goodwin

Recording credit: Dave Celentano, guitar

Cherry Lane Music Company
Director of Publications: Mark Phillips

ISBN 978-1-60378-332-3

Visit our website at www.cherrylaneprint.com

Contents

Introduction

It almost seems as though Joe Bonamassa was destined to reach his current status as one of the most important, influential, and exciting guitarists in the worlds of blues and classic rock. To credit only his unmistakable intangibles, however, is to miss perhaps the essential reason behind his ascent: his tireless work ethic. Yes, his father sold and played guitars and gave him his first axe—a short scale Chiquita—at the age of four. Yes, he acquired the enviable mentors Danny Gatton and B.B. King at ages 11 and 12, respectively, around the time he was beginning middle school. And yes, he clearly had a great deal of innate talent and aptitude for the instrument. But none of these things would really have amounted to much, or allowed him to make the awkward and often precarious transition from child prodigy to adult master, without an absolutely tenacious approach to practice and learning.

Joe has cemented his place in the contemporary guitar strata with a mature and fully realized musical persona that includes not only his phenomenal playing but also great abilities as a singer, songwriter, and charismatic showman. His natural creativity and artistic curiosity were cultivated by people like Gatton, who recognized his affinity for the blues, but encouraged him to constantly broaden his horizons. From jazz to country to early rock 'n' roll, bluegrass, rockabilly, and more—if it was good, it was on the menu. Put on a Bonamassa album and you will surely hear hard-driving blues shuffles and classic rock numbers that were influenced by the British blues greats Joe grew up idolizing; but there's always more. Whether it's a quieter acoustic piece, an impressive slide showcase, or angular, modern fusion playing, he can do it all and loves it all, because he's listened to it all and studied it all, as well.

The 34-year old Bonamassa has come a long way and logged a lot of miles since the early 1990's when he formed Bloodline with Berry Oakley Jr. (son of the late Allman Brothers Band bassist), Erin Davis (the drummer son of the late jazz great Miles Davis), and Waylon Krieger (son of Doors guitarist Robby Krieger). After two albums and a series of tours, the group disbanded, and Joe began his solo career in earnest, releasing a string of highly impressive and steadily evolving albums. These include his debut, *A New Day Yesterday* (2000), *So It's Like That* (2002), *Blues Deluxe* (2003), *Had to Cry Today* (2004), *You & Me* (2006), *Sloe Gin* (2007), *The Ballad of John Henry* (2009), *Black Rock* (2010), and his latest, *Dust Bowl* (2011). The latter two debuted at number one on the Billboard Blues Albums chart (many of the others eventually achieved that position, as well). Bonamassa is also a founding member of the all-star group Black Country Communion with former Deep Purple and Black Sabbath bassist/vocalist Glenn Hughes, Led Zeppelin drummer Jason Bonham, and Dream Theater keyboardist Derek Sherinian. At the time of this writing, they are preparing to embark on a summer tour in support of their upcoming sophomore release, *2*.

In many ways, Bonamassa is a living link between the past and the future of blues and rock guitar. Not only is he knowledgeable of the instrument's traditions and its greatest performers, he has received wisdom and shared personal connections with many legendary blues guitarists. Although he's reverential of the past, he's not a slave to it. His musicality and technical abilities are unquestionably state of the art. He pushes the boundaries of what the guitar can do and raises the standards for the contemporary player ever higher. He is a product of the Internet age and has a ubiquitous web presence that features countless online interviews, YouTube clips, and an excellent personal website. He is still a young man, whose tremendous skill and inquisitiveness will no doubt lead him to new discoveries and new musical terrain. There is much to look forward to in that, both for his fans and for the world of music in general.

In the pages that follow, I'll explore 13 of Joe's hottest and most challenging songs in detail, examining the riffs, licks, and solos that make them so very essential. Much of this material is highly demanding, so get ready to work hard. Be patient and build the trickiest examples up slowly without sacrificing accuracy or musicality. Remember that nothing truly worth having ever comes easy. In the end, I hope you learn as much reading this book as I did writing it.

Gear Notes

Bonamassa has an extensive gear collection, including at least 200 guitars, many of which are rare, vintage models. Unlike many other players, Joe isn't shy about taking them on the road with him—properly protected and heavily insured, of course. His equipment selections change often and have undergone many permutations over his 20-plus years of touring and recording. The list that follows reflects his recent choices and is by no means comprehensive. Nevertheless, it gives you a peek at the tools he employs to craft his diverse and powerful tones. Remember, however, that these are simply tools (okay, really nice tools) and that you're not going to sound like Joe even if your set-up is identical to his. The music is in the individual—not the equipment.

Guitars

Joe no longer plays his Strats very often and is instead closely identified with the Les Paul. He has a number of signature-series Gibson Inspired by Joe Bonamassa Les Pauls equipped with Burst Bucker pickups and hybrid 1958-59 profile necks, in addition to high-end Gibson Custom Shop models and more affordable Epiphone Joe Bonamassa Les Pauls. He has a near-priceless 1959 model that does travel with him, in addition to a '59 reissue (The Gary Moore/Peter Green model), a 1973 Black Les Paul Custom, and the Diet Coke '59 reissue, so named because he bought it on impulse in Japan while pounding the streets in search of a can of his favorite soft drink. That guitar is the one he uses for capoed songs.

Other Gibsons owned by Bonamassa include a 1980s Explorer, a Flying V, and a reissue of a Firebird I from the early '90s (a bit more strident tone…like a Tele, says Bonamassa). A self-proclaimed Freddie King nut, Bonamassa uses a 1973 ES-355 like the one King preferred and also has an extensive collection of hollow- and semi-hollow body Gibsons, running the gamut from 335's (the Lucille model favored by B.B. King) to ES-175's, L-5's, ES-140's, and many more.

Bonamassa is also a big Steve Morse fan and plays the former Dregs guitarist's Ernie Ball/Music Man signature model, as well as that company's John Petrucci Baritone guitar. He also has two custom-made double-necks. One combines a standard six-string with a baritone neck on top, while the other features a 12-string neck and piezo pickup. He also owns various acoustic instruments including guitars, mandolins, and Dobros. In all, Joe travels with about 20 guitars at a time, using about ten in each show. His strings of choice are Ernie Balls, gauged .011 to .052.

Amplifiers

Bonamassa isn't shy about collecting amps either; he owns plenty of unique models and smaller vintage tube amps that he either keeps at home or uses in the studio. He's settled on a touring setup that features four separate amps, two of which are always on at the same time. These include a Marshall Silver Jubilee, a Van Weelden Twinkle Land head (a very nice clone of a Dumble Overdrive Special, says Bonamassa), a Category 5 custom-made head (similar to a Fender Super Lead with an added midrange boost), and a Carol Ann JB-100 head with 6L6 tubes. At times, the Carol Ann is switched out for a Two-Rock Custom Signature Reverb head. Joe feels that no single amp can cover every base and do *everything* well, and says that each also reacts very differently to the touch. Additionally, some clean up quicker at lower volumes than others, providing him with a wide variety of tones and dynamic options. His cabinets are Mojo Musical Supply 4x12's loaded with EV speakers, which are seated atop Auralex Great Grammas risers that lift his cabs from the stage and eliminate unwanted vibrations and other less-than-ideal reactions.

Pedalboard

Bonamassa doesn't always use the same lineup of stompboxes on his pedalboard, but the list usually includes two Voodoo Lab Pedal Power supplies, a Fulltone Tremolo, an Ibanez Tube Screamer (the classic stock pedal), a Boss DD-3 Digital Delay, a Way Huge Pork Loin overdrive, a custom Dunlop Fuzz Face, a Gaspedals Carburetor (overdrive/booster), a Whirlwind selector box, and a Vox wah.

Rack

Some of the components include a Monster Power Conditioner, an EV wireless system, a Peterson VS-R Strobo Rack tuner, a Palmer PDI-03 speaker simulator, a tc electronic 2290 delay and chorus, a Solid State Logic XLogic Alpha Channel preamp for use with acoustic guitar, and a Diaz Vibramaster, which supplies classic tube reverb, tremolo, and vibrato.

Additionally, Bonamassa uses a Moog Theremin on a few songs to create eerie, otherworldly sound effects such as those heard on "The Ballad of John Henry." The Theremin runs through a Boss delay and an Ernie Ball volume pedal.

A Note on "Position Playing"

Throughout this book, you will find numerous references to left-hand (fretting-hand) positioning. For example, you may read: Begin in 5th position, then slide up to 12th position to bend the B string at the 14th fret with your ring finger. What exactly does this mean? Simply put, position is determined by whatever fret your index finger happens to be on. In this case, your index finger would be on the 5th fret, your middle finger on the 6th, ring finger on the 7th, and pinky on the 8th fret. When you slide up to 12th position, with your index finger now on the 12th fret, your ring finger will naturally line up with the 14th fret and perform the aforementioned bend. However, just because you are in, say, 5th position, it doesn't necessarily mean that you have to play any notes on the 5th fret. If your ring finger and pinky moved back and forth between the 7th and 8th frets, you'd still be in 5th position. When you play a standard, open-strings version of a G major chord, you are in 2nd position, because, while your middle finger will play the root on the low E string's 3rd fret, your index finger will be on the 2nd fret of the A string (playing the B).

Why all this stress on fingering positions? Because they're essential to playing the guitar effectively, and to playing the music of Joe Bonamassa, specifically. Much of his work is difficult to pull off in the best of circumstances, and if the wrong fingers or fingering combinations are used, you're toast—you won't be able to do it. You might get through a lick slowly and sloppily, but you won't be playing "Revenge of the 10 Gallon Hat" or "Blues Deluxe" at full speed like that. The licks in these songs (and others) feature constant positional shifts that will take you up and down the fretboard in mere moments, often in the course of a single phrase. So even if you know these songs and licks extremely well, take the time to read through the accompanying instructional paragraphs and check out the fingerings and positions detailed in them. They'll make all the difference in the world.

About the Author

Toby Wine is a native New Yorker and a freelance guitarist, composer, arranger, and educator. He is a graduate of the Manhattan School of Music, where he studied composition with Manny Albam and Edward Green. Toby has performed with Philip Harper (of the Harper Brothers and Art Blakey's Jazz Messengers), Bob Mover, Ari Ambrose, Michael and Carolyn Leonhart (of Steely Dan), Peter Hartmann, Ian Hendrickson-Smith (of Sharon Jones and the Dap-Kings), Melee, Saycon (*Fela!*), Nakia Henry, and the Harlem-based rock band Kojomodibo Sun, among others. His arrangements and compositions can be heard on recordings by Tobias Gebb and Unit Seven (*Free at Last*), Phillip Harper (*Soulful Sin, The Thirteenth Moon*, Muse Records), Ari Ambrose (*Early Song*, Steeplechase), and Ian Hendrickson-Smith (*Up in Smoke*, Sharp Nine). Toby leads his own trio and septet, does studio sessions, and works as a sideman with a variety of tri-state area bandleaders. He spent four years as the music librarian for the Carnegie Hall Jazz Band and is currently an instructor at the Church Street School for Music and Art in Tribeca. He is the author of numerous Cherry Lane publications, including *The Art of Texas Blues, 150 Cool Jazz Licks in Tab, Johnny Winter Plays the Blues, Steely Dan: Legendary Licks,* and *Derek Trucks: Legendary Licks.*

Acknowledgments

Many thanks are due to Cherry Lane's fearless leaders, John Stix and Mark Phillips, and to Susan Poliniak, for her insight, guidance, and continued support over the last decade. Thanks also to my parents, Rosemary and Jerry, and to Christina, Bibi, Bob, Jack, Noah, Enid, Mover, Humph (R.I.P.), fellow author Karl Kaminski, and all the great teachers—and students—I've had. I've learned so much from all of you.

Miss You, Hate You

From *A New Day Yesterday* (2000)

Words and Music by Joe Bonamassa and Richard Feldman

TRACK 01 Tuning track (standard tuning)

Let's begin by taking a detailed look at this catchy, southern-rock-flavored song from Joe Bonamassa's debut album. The simple structure and G-major-based chord progressions allow Joe plenty of space for both soulful singing and expressive soloing—particularly over the long E-minor vamp near the song's end. "It took me 45 minutes to write, and to this day it's the closest thing I've ever had to a hit," Bonamassa says. "There's an 82-bar solo at the end. So I wasn't looking particularly for radio."

Intro Riff

This riff serves as both intro and accompaniment to the verses in a somewhat simplified form. It's a bit harder than it looks (and sounds) in that there's extensive string-skipping involved, so you'll want to slow it down a bit and practice it carefully before you build back up to full tempo. The left hand has the easier job here, as you move between standard G, Em, and C chord shapes, as well as a first-inversion D chord (with F♯ in the bass on the low E string). The sliding double-stops in the fourth measure should be played with your index and middle fingers on the B and G strings, respectively.

TRACK 02

Interlude Lick

This short, tasty phrase is played between the first and second verses of the song and features smooth and subtle use of the whammy bar, although it can be easily played on a fixed bridge (non-tremolo) guitar, as well. In this case, simply use your index finger to slide up and down the G string in measures 1 and 3 on a single pick-stroke, and play the other notes as indicated. If using the bar, depress it for each indication to sound the pitch. The 10th-fret, B-string bends should be played by the ring finger, with the other fingers lined up behind it to aid in the push and ensure accurate intonation.

TRACK 03

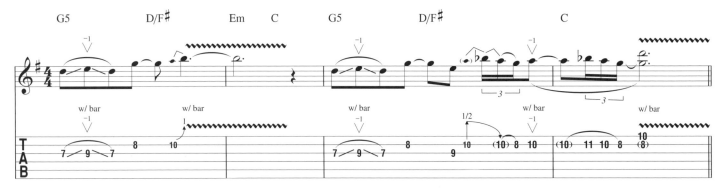

Solo

The excerpt below includes all of Joe's 10-bar solo following the song's second chorus. Begin by sliding up the D string to the 9th fret with your ring finger, then shift into 8th position to grab the G on the B string's 8th fret with your index finger. All of the 10th-fret bends in the first two measures should be played by the ring finger. There's a temporary drop down into 5th position in measure 3 before Joe climbs back up the neck into 12th position during measures 5 and 6. The final four measures find Joe leaving the G major pentatonic scale behind and shifting to G minor pentatonic to play over the B♭ and C chords, working in a few tricky little positional slides and a handful of *overbends* (raising the B♭ on the B string's 11th fret two whole steps to D, and the 7th-fret G-string D up a step and a half to F). He also includes both E and A in these licks, representing the raised 11th and major 7th of the B♭ chord, respectively, and suggesting the G Dorian mode.

(Slow demo, 0:34)

TRACK 04

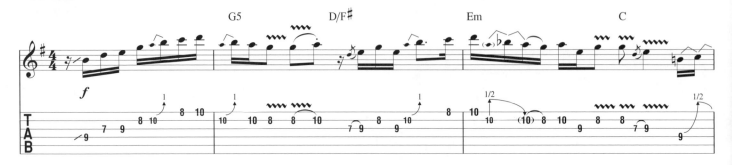

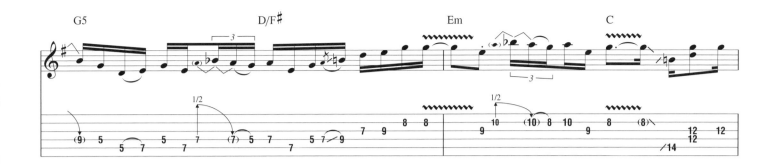

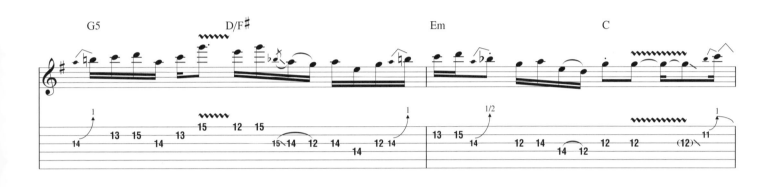

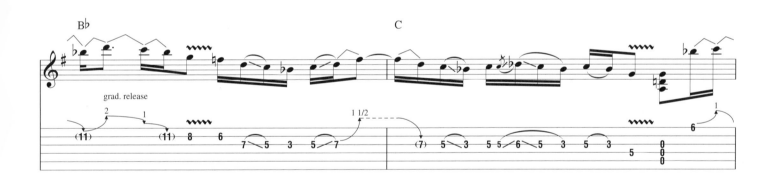

Outro Solo Excerpt #1

"Miss You, Hate You" ends with the previously mentioned jam in E minor, in which Joe really stretches out with playing that runs the gamut from angular, fusion-like lines to classic blues-rock phrasing. The first excerpt from this section begins with a ringing triplet phrase in which the middle finger plays the C on the A string, and the index finger performs the pull-off from the 2nd fret to the open high E string. All bends in this excerpt should be played by the middle finger.

The low C and high F♯ against the E played by the bass imply an Emin9♭6 chord, a particularly evocative and sophisticated harmony for what began as a toe-tapping, sing-along classic-rock song. It's the first clear demonstration of Joe's flagrant disregard for stylistic or genre rules among many that we will encounter in the pages of this book. He's always tasty and plays in keeping with the feeling and mood of the song, but he doesn't confine himself artificially by obeying predetermined limits set by himself or anyone else. That's a useful lesson for any artist concerned with originality and self-expression.

TRACK 05

Outro Solo Excerpt #2

The next excerpt begins with the droning, open low E string, followed by a 7th-position phrase in which the index finger is used to barre the D, G, and B strings at the 7th fret. In the second measure, extend your ring finger to play the G on the A string's 10th fret, then slide down to the 9th-fret F♯ at the end of beat 2. Follow the let ring indications carefully here.

TRACK 06 (Slow demo, 0:11)

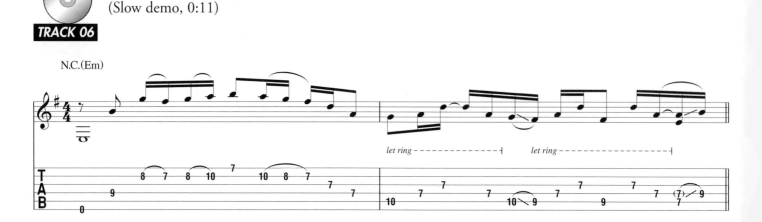

Outro Solo Excerpt #3

Our next example begins in 15th position and features ring finger bends on both the high E and B strings' 17th frets in the opening measure. Measure 2 starts with another ring-finger bend on the B string; perform the A-string slides that follow with the same finger while your index finger takes the G-string notes a 6th above. This puts you in position to use your index finger for the sliding phrase that begins measure 3 and works its way down to the open low E string at the end of the excerpt.

(Slow demo, 0:17)

TRACK 07

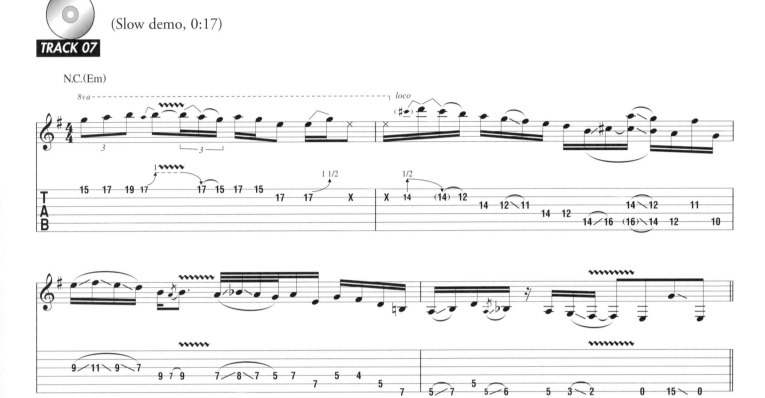

Outro Solo Excerpt #4

Begin the phrase below with your pinky, index, and middle fingers on the D, G, and B strings, respectively, letting the strings ring freely for the first three beats of the measure. On beat 4, drop down and use your ring finger to slide up the A string to the 14th fret. In measure 2, the G-string notes should be played by the index finger, while the A-string notes should be taken by the middle or ring finger, depending on whether they are one or two frets higher than the G-string notes. In either case, flatten the lower finger slightly to prevent the open D string from ringing when the parallel 6ths are struck simultaneously. The second half of the phrase features a particularly cool lick combining open and fretted strings in sextuplets played fast enough that they are nearly—but not quite—tremolo picked. Be sure to keep the rhythms accurate here.

(Slow demo, 0:17)

TRACK 08

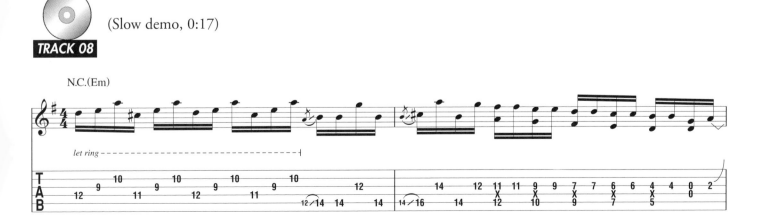

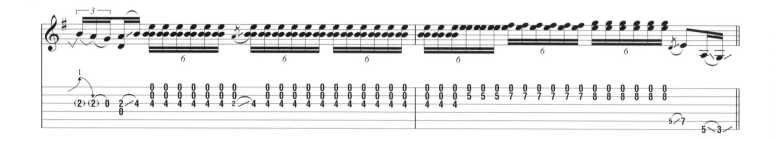

Outro Solo Excerpt #5

Our final example from this song contrasts riffy chord phrases in measures 1 and 3 with lightning-fast single-note lines in measures 2 and 4. The descending lick in the second measure should be played in 1st position, so that the ring finger pulls off to the open B string and the middle finger takes all 2nd-fret notes. In measure 4, slide into 12th position with your index finger and stay there for the duration. This is not a particularly challenging phrase if you play it at half speed or use hammer-ons and pull-offs. If you can play this one along with Joe at full tempo, picking every note accurately, kudos to you—you're one hell of a picker! The rest of us will want to work this over slowly, building up speed over time. These kind of chops don't develop overnight, so be patient, and put in your work in the woodshed. You'll get there eventually.

(Slow demo, 0:17)

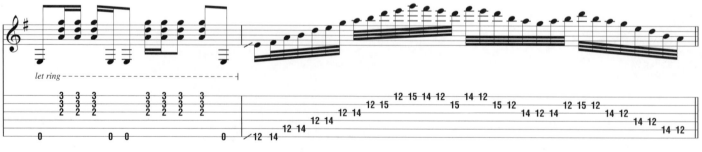

If Heartaches Were Nickels

From *A New Day Yesterday* (2000)

Words and Music by Warren Haynes

 Tuning track (standard tuning, down 1/2 step; low to high: E♭-A♭-D♭-G♭-B♭-E♭)

TRACK 10

This slow, searing 12/8 blues in A minor comes from the pen of Gov't Mule and Allman Brothers Band guitar whiz Warren Haynes and features the great Gregg Allman on vocals and organ. It's the perfect vehicle for Bonamassa to demonstrate his awe-inspiring command of both traditional and contemporary blues and rock soloing and the unique spin he brings to the genre. His solo is broken down below into four-measure excerpts, which are played over the first, second, and third four-measure segments of the 12-bar form. Joe tunes down a half step on this one, so be sure to lower each string (E♭-A♭-D♭-G♭-B♭-E♭, low to high) if you're going to play along with the recording. While the majority of the solo licks are built on notes from the A minor pentatonic scale, take note of the various extensions employed along the way that add subtle shading to the proceedings. Joe's slick, position-shifting moves allow him to play both vertically *and* horizontally with ease and are also of particular interest to anyone looking to open up the neck and break out of standard blues-box playing.

Solo, Measures 1–4 (Chorus 2)

Joe opens his second solo chorus with a sustained step-and-a-half bend on the high E string, pushing E up a minor 3rd to G at the 12th fret. After finishing out the measure in 10th position, he slides up the neck quickly and lands in 17th position, using the A minor pentatonic blues box on the highest reaches of the neck. The remainder of the example is played in this area and features a number of overbends, all of which should be played with the ring finger.

 (Slow demo, 0:27)

TRACK 11

Tune down 1/2 step:
(low to high) E♭-A♭-D♭-G♭-B♭-E♭

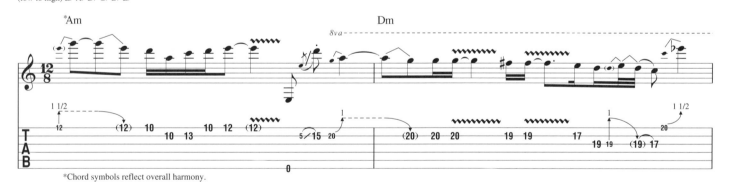

*Chord symbols reflect overall harmony.

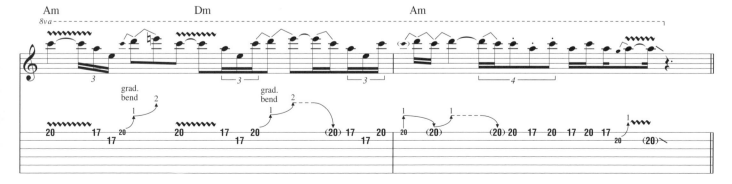

Solo, Measures 1-4 (Chorus 3)

The next excerpt begins the third chorus with a pickup played in 7th position. End the pickup by sliding up the G string with your index finger so that the first measure begins with your middle finger bending the B string up a minor 3rd (with help from the index finger lined up behind it). The next phrase is played in the standard 5th-position A minor pentatonic fingering, with 7th- and 8th-fret ring finger bends on the B and high E strings. There's a tricky little maneuver in measure 2 that begins with a ring finger slide up the G string to the 9th fret, and a double bend on the B string with the same finger, followed by a slide down to the 8th fret. Next, play the eight notes on the G string with a single pick stroke, using an overdriven tone to provide the necessary sustain. Most of the remaining notes can be played in the 5th-position A minor pentatonic fingering. Bonamassa adds color to his lines by employing the 9th (B) liberally throughout the excerpt.

 (Slow demo, 0:28)

TRACK 12

Tune down 1/2 step:
(low to high) Eb-Ab-Db-Gb-Bb-Eb

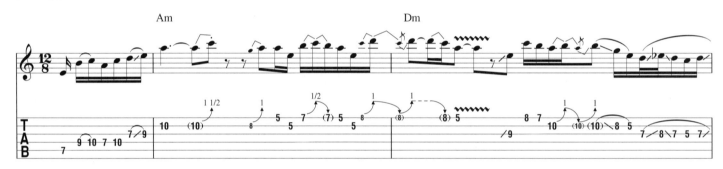

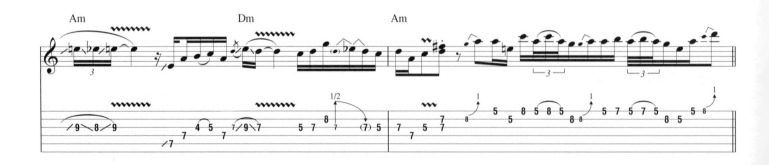

Solo, Measures 1-4 (Chorus 4)

The final solo chorus begins with a series of phrases played in the upper reaches of the neck that require a deft, agile touch. Space is at a premium here, and the notes go by at a rapid-fire pace—particularly towards the end of the excerpt. The good news is that the bulk of the playing is done in the standard A minor pentatonic fingering, and there are no particularly odd positional shifts or unorthodox techniques. The real challenge, then, is to bring the licks up to speed gradually and to play them authoritatively with *rhythmic accuracy*. Joe's not just spraying notes around as if he's wielding an Uzi; each lick is in the pocket and played with deadly precision.

 (Slow demo, 0:27)

Tune down 1/2 step:
(low to high) Eb-Ab-Db-Gb-Bb-Eb

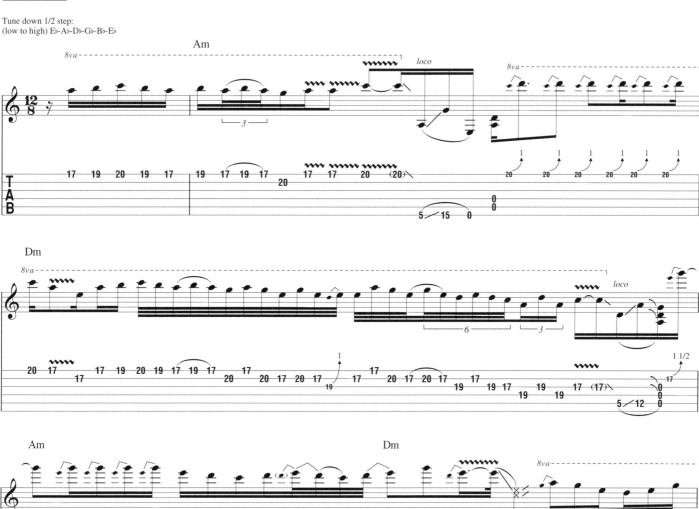

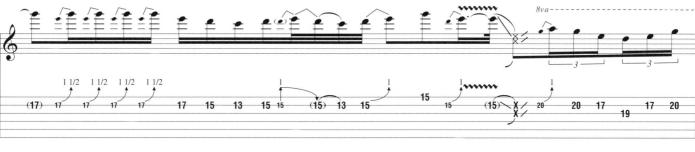

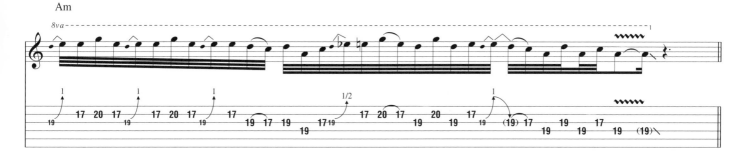

Solo, Measures 5–8 (Chorus 1)

The next three examples are played over the middle portion of the form, as the chords move up to the IV (D minor). This one is full of soaring bends, each of which should be played by the ring finger. Stay in 10th position for most of the phrase, moving up the neck in the final measure to grab the 15th-fret notes on the high E string with your pinky.

 (Slow demo, 0:27)

Tune down 1/2 step:
(low to high) Eb-Ab-Db-Gb-Bb-Eb

Solo, Measures 5–8 (Chorus 3)

Begin the next lick by bending the high E string up a whole step with your ring finger, then catch both the E *and* B strings with the same finger for the second bend. Near the end of the opening measure, move up two frets to bend the G string at the 9th fret with your ring finger, then use the slide from fret 7 to fret 5 return to the 5th-position pentatonic fingering for the hammer-on/pull-off lick on beat 3 of the second measure. The slides between the 7th and 9th frets in measures 2 and 3 should be played by the ring finger as well.

 (Slow demo, 0:27)

Tune down 1/2 step:
(low to high) Eb-Ab-Db-Gb-Bb-Eb

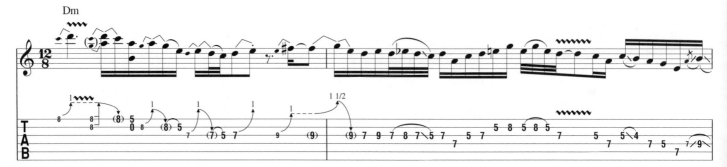

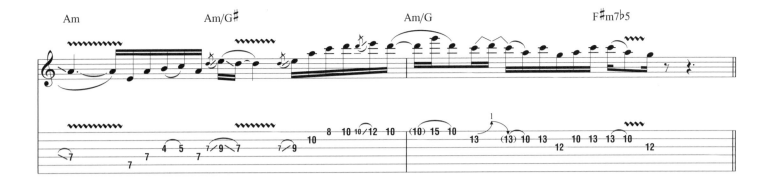

Solo, Measures 5-8 (Chorus 4)

The next excerpt is particularly tricky because it's quite fast and requires a number of slick shifts of position. Begin on the 5th fret, using A pentatonic fingering, and perform the first two bends with the ring finger. Use your middle finger to play the D note on the G string, 7th fret, and to slide up to the 9th fret. Then use your ring finger to slide up the high E string from the 10th to the 12th fret, putting you in 10th position, and use the same finger to reach up to the 15th fret near the end of the measure. From here you can finish out much of the phrase in 12th position. Cap things off with the sliding, tremolo-picked double-stops and a final flurry that takes you up into 17th position for a series of wailing 20th-fret bends. Take your time with this one—there's a lot going on here!

(Slow demo, 0:27)

Tune down 1/2 step:
(low to high) E♭-A♭-D♭-G♭-B♭-E♭

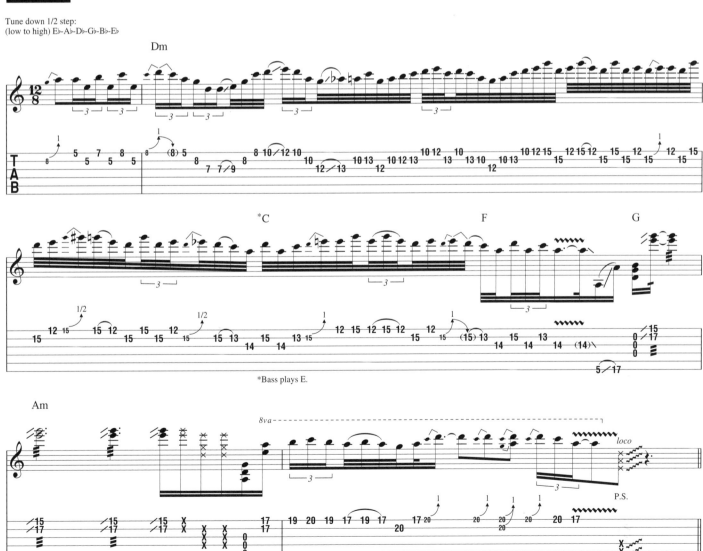

Solo, Measures 9–12 (Chorus 1)

The following turnaround phrase begins on the ♭VI chord (Fmaj7) rather than the V (E), but its highly pentatonic nature allows it to be employed over standard blues-turnaround progressions as well. Start by sliding up the B string an octave to the 17th-fret with your index finger, and perform all bends in the first measure with your ring finger. You may need to experiment a bit to accurately recreate the pitches of the pick harmonics that follow on the A string; try varying your pick placement between the bridge and the end of the neck until you get the harmonic tones indicated by the diamond-shaped noteheads. The second half of the phrase is played in 10th position and features a 13th-fret whole-step bend pushed even further until the initial note (C) rises a major 3rd to E. Overbends like these (and the bend on the high E string that follows) are a staple of Bonamassa's solo style and require a fair amount of finger strength to accomplish. Remember to use your index and middle fingers, lined up on the bending string behind the ring finger, to assist in the push. Most importantly, hit your marks—an out of tune bend will leave you sounding like an amateur at open-mic night.

 (Slow demo, 0:27)

TRACK 17

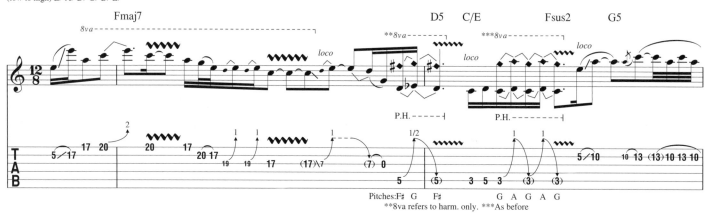

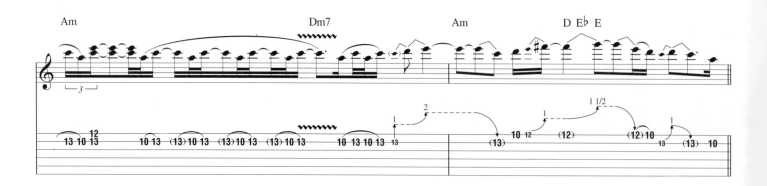

Solo, Measures 9-12 (Chorus 3)

The following turnaround is also played over the ♭VI chord and includes the rising progression in measure 2 (D5, C/E, Fsus2, and G5), also encountered in the previous example. These chords are used to provide a richer harmonic background over which to solo. They don't alter the essential A minor tonality, which means these licks can be employed in a variety of blues and rock settings once you've gotten them under your fingers. This one starts with a ring-finger bend on the B string (15th fret), with the pinky grabbing the G on the high E string's 15th fret. At the end of the first measure, shift upwards into 17th position and rake across the strings, with your index finger barring the 17th fret to begin the next phrase. The second half of the excerpt drops down into 5th position for some classic A minor pentatonic moves.

(Slow demo, 0:27)

TRACK 18

Solo, Measures 9-12 (Chorus 4)

This excerpt brings a fiery end to the solo and begins over the more conventional v chord (Em) this time. The moves are similar to the previous example, with rapid-fire 17th-position licks in the first measure that descend into 13th position in measure 2 via the repeated step-and-a-half B-string bends and the 15th-fret bends with the pinky on the high E string. The second half of the phrase drops down into the 5th-position A minor pentatonic scale for a flurry of bends and pull-offs before coming to a close by ascending chromatically to the D that begins the bridge section. Once again, try to find that F♯ harmonic by varying the placement of your pick to change the harmonic pitch.

(Slow demo, 0:27)

TRACK 19

Tune down 1/2 step:
(low to high) E♭-A♭-D♭-G♭-B♭-E♭

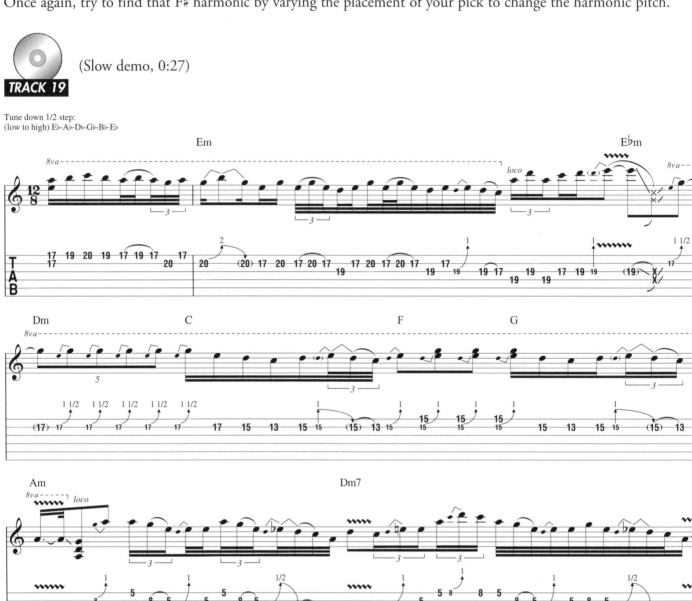

Pitch: F♯
*8va refers to harm. only.

My Mistake

From *So It's Like That* (2002)

Words and Music by Joe Bonamassa and Mark Lizotte

Tuning track (Drop D tuning, down 1/2 step;
low to high: D♭-A♭-D♭-G♭-B♭-E♭)

TRACK 20

The opening number on Bonamassa's second studio album demonstrates Joe's penchant for crafting catchy, concise, classic-rock songs that are clearly more than just vehicles for his impressive solos. A number of guitars are employed, including acoustics and electrics in drop-D tuning lowered to D♭ (D♭-A♭-D♭-G♭-B♭-E♭, low to high) and an additional electric tuned down a half step (E♭-A♭-D♭-G♭-B♭-E♭) for the solo licks and fills. Be sure to make all the necessary tuning adjustments before you get started on this one.

Intro Riff

This four-measure phrase is played first by a solo-acoustic steel-string and then by an electric guitar once the entire band kicks into gear. The drop-tuning allows for rich, full chord voicings that not only sound great, but are easy to play as well. The same riff also serves as accompaniment to the song's chorus.

TRACK 21

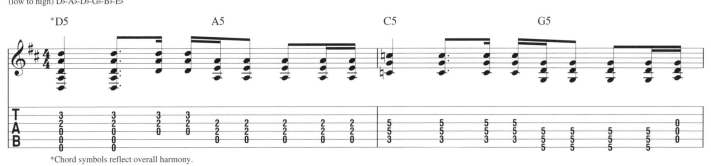

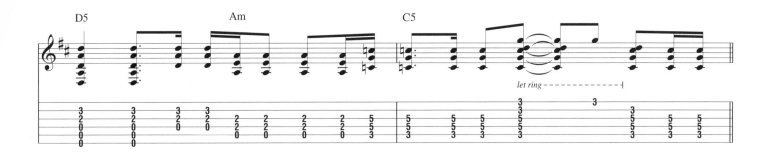

Intro Fill

This simple lick mirrors the chorus melody closely and is played smoothly with a distinctively vocal quality. Begin in 7th position so that your ring finger plays the 9th-fret E on the G string that slides both down to the 7th fret and up to the 12th fret. You'll need to make a quick shift in measure 2 to bend the G string with your ring finger as well.

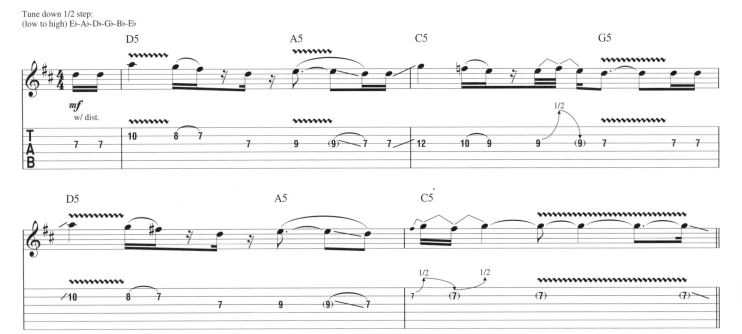

Single-Note Intro Riff

This short 16th-note lick immediately precedes Joe's vocal entrance. Barre the 5th fret with your index finger and use your ring finger to get to the 7th-fret notes and bends in the first measure. Use the same fingering up three frets in measure 2. The real challenge here lies in the extensive string-skipping, so pick your way through it carefully. Observe the palm-mute indications, let everything ring throughout each measure, and try to capture Joe's gentle, subdued vibe, as well.

 (Slow demo, 0:14)

Drop D tuning, down 1/2 step:
(low to high) Db-Ab-Db-Gb-Bb-Eb

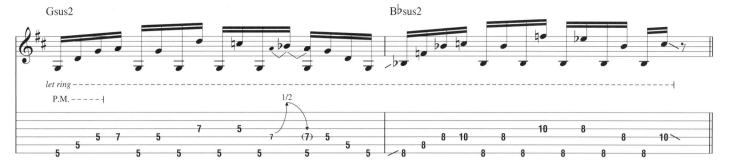

Solo Excerpt #1

This sweetly melodic lick mimics the chorus vocal an octave higher, beginning on the 17th fret of the high E string. The second measure starts with a ring-finger bend at the B string's 18th fret, followed by a 15th-fret index-finger bend. Stay in this position so that the ring finger takes the 17th-fret, B-string bend in measure 3 while the pinky gets to the A on the high E string. Finally, shift up in the last measure to play the half-step bends with your ring finger as you finish out the excerpt.

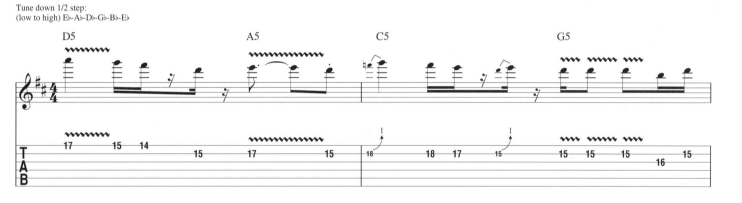

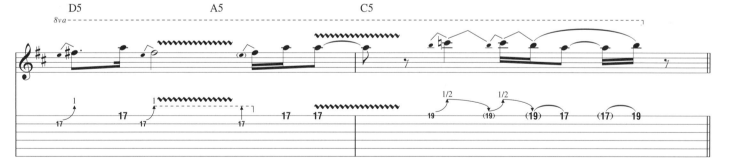

Solo Excerpt #2

The next lick follows immediately on the heels of the previous example. Each of the three hammer-on/pull-off/slide groupings in the first measure should be initiated by the ring finger, with the index finger performing the slides that shift you down the neck. Begin the second measure by bending the B string with your ring finger, while your pinky gets to the A on the high E string above. The ring finger should also perform the 18th-fret overbend at the end of measure 3.

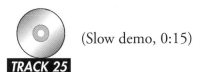 (Slow demo, 0:15)

Tune down 1/2 step:
(low to high) Eb-Ab-Db-Gb-Bb-Eb

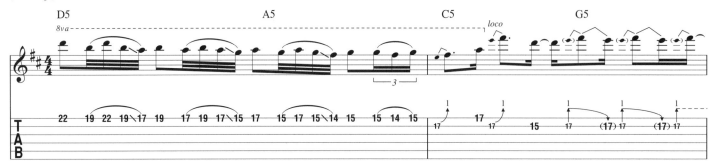

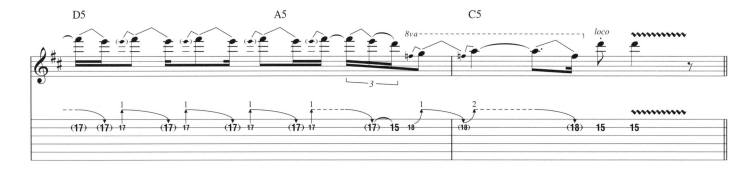

Solo Excerpt #3

Here's a short-but-sweet, rapid-fire 32nd-note lick that occurs near the end of the song. It's played entirely in 14th position, so that your index finger takes all the 14th-fret notes and your pinky (don't use your ring finger here) handles all the 17th-fret notes. Note that Joe picks every note in the line, avoiding hammer-ons and pull-offs entirely. It's an easy passage to play at half-speed, but it's very challenging at the original tempo. If nothing else, it makes a fine picking exercise and gives you a goal to shoot for as you seek to improve your alternate picking chops. Practice it slow enough that you can play it cleanly. Don't increase the speed until you can do so comfortably and without any hitches in your technique.

 (Slow demo, 0:07)

Tune down 1/2 step:
(low to high) Eb-Ab-Db-Gb-Bb-Eb

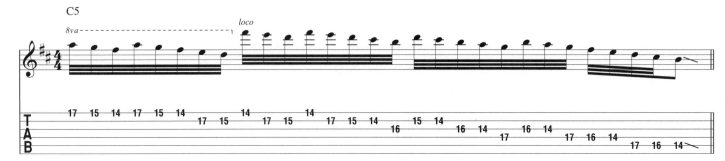

So It's Like That

From *So It's Like That* (2002)

Words and Music by Joe Bonamassa and Michael Himelstein

This hard-charging blues in B has a distinct Texas flavor, showing the influence of Stevie Ray Vaughan and earlier practitioners such as Freddie King and Albert Collins. It's a straight-ahead, no-nonsense example of the style, but Bonamassa puts his stamp on it, letting his personality shine through on both guitar and vocals. Be sure to tune down a half step (Eb-Ab-Db-Gb-Bb-Eb, low to high) if you're going to play along with the recording, and don't miss the intriguing chord substitutions employed in both the verse and solo sections. Joe recorded this one (on an Eric Clapton signature Strat) after a wine-fueled dinner and calls it a drunken swagger tune. See if you can capture a bit of that swagger for yourself.

Verse Riff

This predominantly single-note riff serves as accompaniment to the vocal and is typical of the style, with the bass guitar tracking the line closely an octave below. Instead of moving to the IV chord in measure 5, the harmony shifts to the III (D7), while the turnaround descends to the bVI (G7) before moving on to the V (F#7) and bVII (A7) chords in measure 10. There's a classic turnaround phrase in the last two measures that every blues guitarist should know.

TRACK 27

Tune down 1/2 step:
(low to high) Eb-Ab-Db-Gb-Bb-Eb

*Shuffle feel applies to all examples in this chapter.

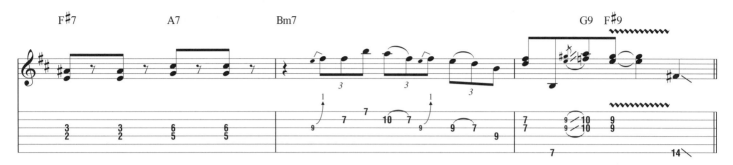

Solo Chorus # 1

The opening chorus of Joe's solo begins in 7th position and remains there for the majority of its 12 bars, although there's a quick downshift at the end of measure 7 and a rise to 10th position in measure 9. Note the changes to the chord progression during the solos: the standard IV chord (E7) is now employed in measures 5 and 6, while the turn-around simply shifts up to the III (D7) for two measures, rather than the ♭VI-V-♭VII progression employed in the verses. Bonamassa plays strictly from the B and D pentatonic scales throughout the example.

(Slow demo, 0:26)

Tune down 1/2 step:
(low to high) E♭-A♭-D♭-G♭-B♭-E♭

Solo Chorus #2

Chorus 2 opens with repeated double-stops on the B and high E strings (use your middle and ring fingers, respectively, and bend them slightly towards the ceiling as indicated). Move to 12th position at the end of measure 4 for the E7 licks that outline the harmony and feature a number of chromatic passing tones, before returning to 7th position in measures 7 and 8. Joe creates a lot of interest by augmenting his pentatonic licks with the E7 shapes in the example—it's a refreshing change from simply wailing on the pentatonic scale, and it's true to the style as well.

(Slow demo, 0:26)

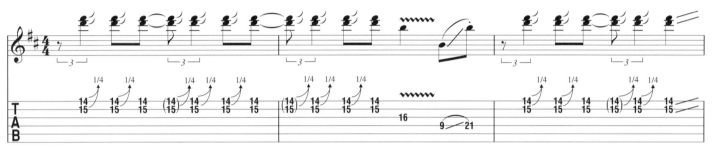

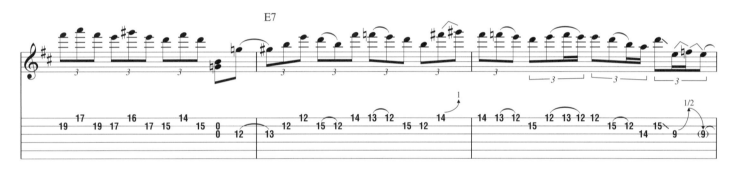

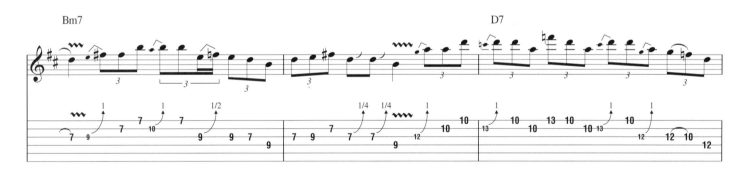

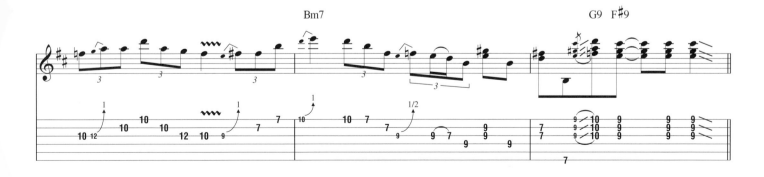

Solo Chorus #3

Joe's third chorus begins in similar fashion, with repeated double-stops on the top two strings, answered this time by vibrato-laden quarter-note triplets on a high B. By the end of measure 5, he has returned to his B minor pentatonic phrases, moving everything up three frets in measures 9 and 10 to tackle the D7 chord in the same way. His re-use of earlier melodic material only serves to strengthen the entire solo, providing cohesion and a sense of unity. If you have a great idea, use it and use it again—don't just toss it out until it's been thoroughly explored and exploited.

 (Slow demo, 0:26)

TRACK 30

Tune down 1/2 step:
(low to high) E♭-A♭-D♭-G♭-B♭-E♭

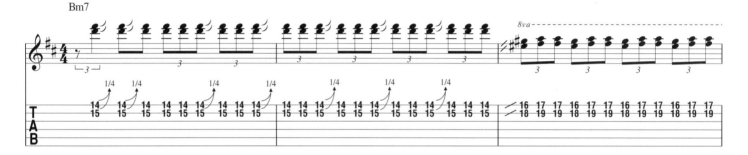

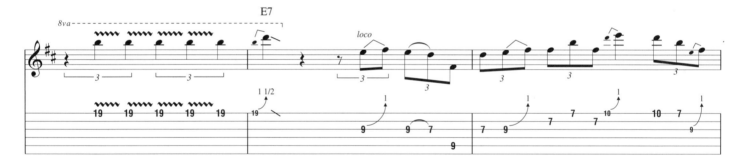

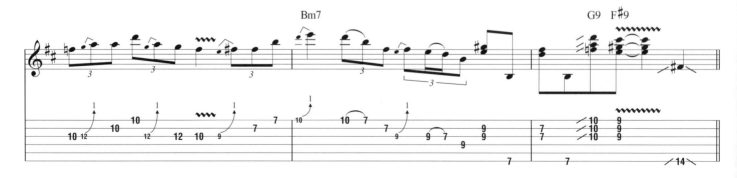

Pain and Sorrow

From *So It's Like That* (2002)   Words and Music by Joe Bonamassa, Richard Feldman and Eric Pressly

Tuning track (standard tuning, down 1 step;
low to high: D-G-C-F-A-D)

TRACK 31

This 10-minute opus is truly epic. It's so jam-packed with phenomenal guitar playing that it could serve as the basis for an entire book by itself. Bonamassa demonstrates not only his supreme command of the instrument, but also his masterful control of sounds and textures, employing a wide variety of effects to create a whole world of stunning sonic landscapes. Choosing examples from "Pain and Sorrow" was no easy task—it's all challenging, fun, and educational—but we did it nonetheless, cherry-picking the crucial riffs and licks. The following excerpts take a look at some of the best moments from this treasure trove of guitar wizardry. Joe tunes down a whole step for this one, so drop your strings accordingly (D-G-C-F-A-D, low to high) before you get started.

Verse Riff

After an eerie intro laden with volume swells and resonant feedback, the band kicks in with this hard-rocking riff in the Hendrix/Stevie Ray mold. It's the easiest part of the song to play—just use your index finger to get to the D on the 5th fret of the A string throughout the phrase, and play the trill in the second measure by hammering on and pulling off rapidly between your index and ring fingers. In the final measure, slide up to the 12th-fret E minor pentatonic fingering and bend the G string at the 14th fret with your ring finger.

TRACK 32

Tune down 1 step:
(low to high) D-G-C-F-A-D

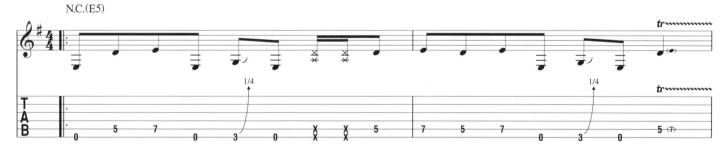

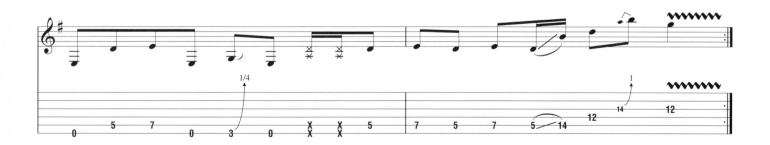

Solo Excerpt # 1

After the first three minutes of the song, Joe begins an extended solo that runs throughout the rest of the tune. Approximate timings are given for the excerpted licks that follow, beginning with the phrase below that occurs at 3:37. It stays strictly in 12th position, with the ring finger playing all the bends. Dig the held bend in measure 2, to which Joe adds his pinky on the high E string above, a country-guitar staple given new life via a fresh injection of tube-driven overdrive.

TRACK 33

Tune down 1 step:
(low to high) D-G-C-F-A-D

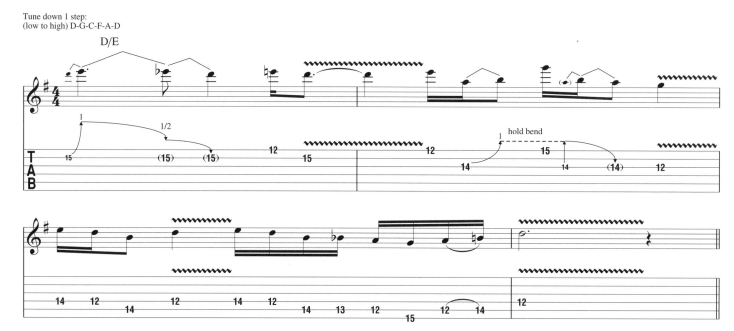

Solo Excerpt # 2

The next lick, occurring at the 4:04 mark of the song, also stays in 12th position until the very end, at which point the A on the low E string at the 17th fret is bent up a whole step to B by pulling towards the floor. The notes are all taken from the E minor pentatonic scale, with the exception of the F♯ in measure 4 (the 9th of the E chord) and the flatted 5th (B♭) later in the same measure. The lick derives much of its powerful impact from its rhythmic intensity and Joe's monstrous tone.

(Slow demo, 0:15)

TRACK 34

Tune down 1 step:
(low to high) D-G-C-F-A-D

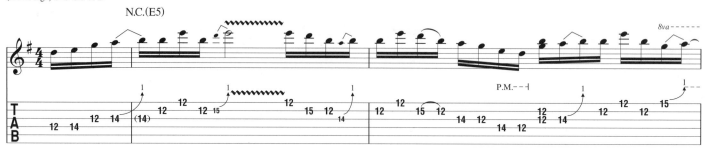

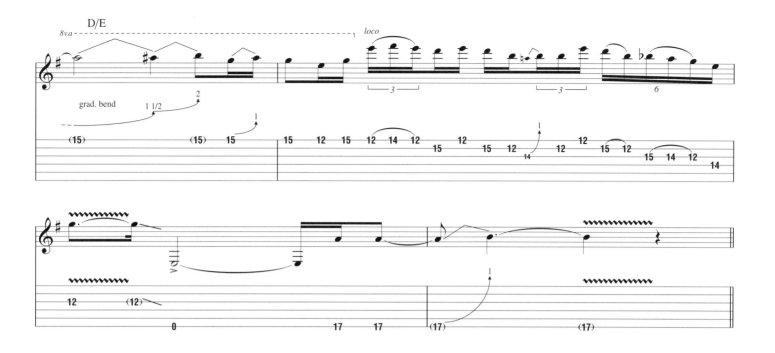

Solo Excerpt #3

Here's another short phrase demonstrating Bonamassa's mastery of all things pentatonic. He kicks things off with an *oblique* bend in which the ring finger pushes the G string up a whole step while the pinky remains stationery on the B string above. Occurring at the 4:30 mark, it's another example of the power of Joe's rhythmic command. It's the same E minor pentatonic scale everyone at the local open mic plays every night across the country. They're just not doing it with the same level of rhythmic precision. The same can be said of many other master players: Clapton, Hendrix, Duane Allman, Stevie Ray, etc. They're all playing the same notes as the rest of us, but they each exhibit highly individualistic, extremely musical phrasing and a rhythmic sensibility that's always on time and in the pocket. Don't overlook this most crucial aspect of creating and organizing a truly memorable solo.

TRACK 35

Tune down 1 step:
(low to high) D-G-C-F-A-D

Solo Excerpt #4

The lick below (4:45) alternates between three-note groupings played on the top three strings—with the middle finger bending the G string and the ring finger and pinky on the B and high E strings—and booming rhythmic punctuations on the open low E string. The initial idea is repeated three times with slight variations and answered by a new idea in measure 4. It's a highly effective method for organizing melodic material in an improvised solo. Joe is clearly doing this instinctively here, without premeditation, but it's a useful technique to try consciously as you begin to build your own solo style.

(Slow demo, 0:11)

TRACK 36

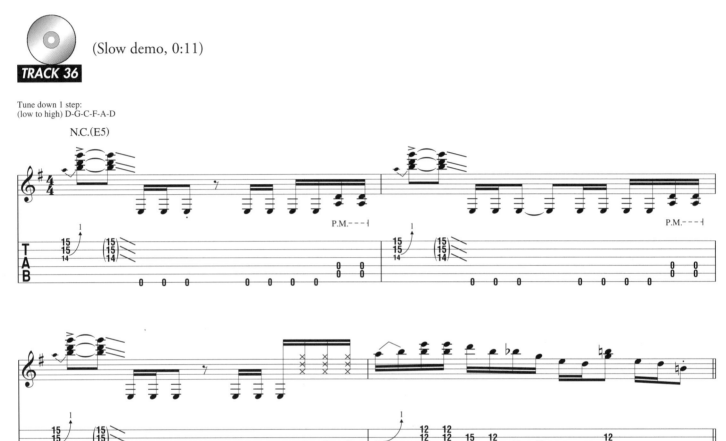

Solo Excerpt #5

The longer, wah-laden lick below occurs at the five-minute mark and features some truly blazing lines and challenging rhythmic combinations. The groups of seven and five in measures 4 and 5 are difficult enough, but are made even more so by their close proximity to sextuplet groupings in the line. Needless to say, this is one that will likely require some serious work to pull off accurately and confidently. Stay in 12th position until measure 6, when you'll need to perform each downward slide on the G string with your index finger, eventually pulling off to the open string and finishing the measure by bending the string up a whole step at the 2nd fret. While there's a lot of repetition in the phrase, don't gloss over the tricky rhythms and subtle intricacies here; take your time and learn to play it right. For an added challenge, plug in your wah-wah pedal and see if you can cop Joe's carefully nuanced sweeps across the frequency spectrum. They really elevate the licks to another level of dramatic, psychedelic intensity.

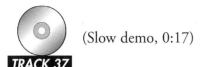

(Slow demo, 0:17)

Tune down 1 step:
(low to high) D-G-C-F-A-D

N.C.(E5)

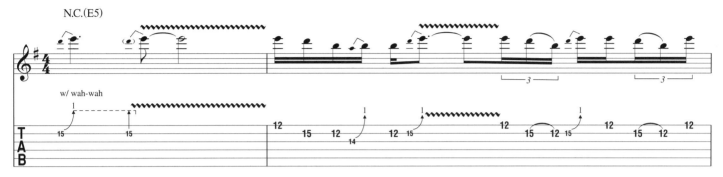

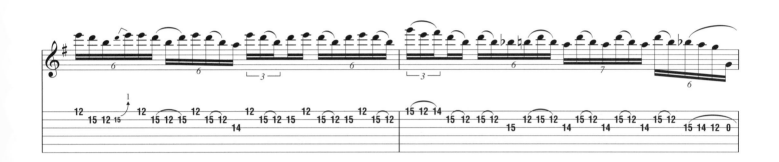

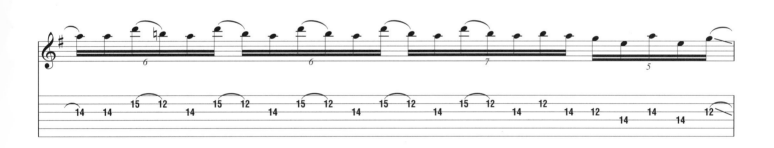

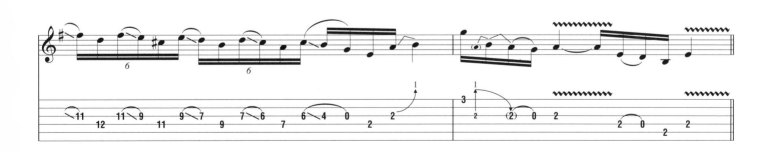

Solo Excerpt #6

We now jump ahead to the 7:46 mark for a six-measure phrase in which Joe employs repetition to great effect. There isn't a hammer-on or pull-off in sight, so get ready to put your picking chops to the test. You'll need to take your time getting this one up to speed. It's all 12th-position E minor pentatonic playing (with the exception of the F#s added in the first measure), so fingering will not be an issue. Instead, the challenge lies in being rhythmically accurate—particularly in measure 1, with the five-, six-, and seven-note combinations, and in the sheer speed of the alternate picking required to play this one at full tempo. Good luck!

 (Slow demo, 0:15)

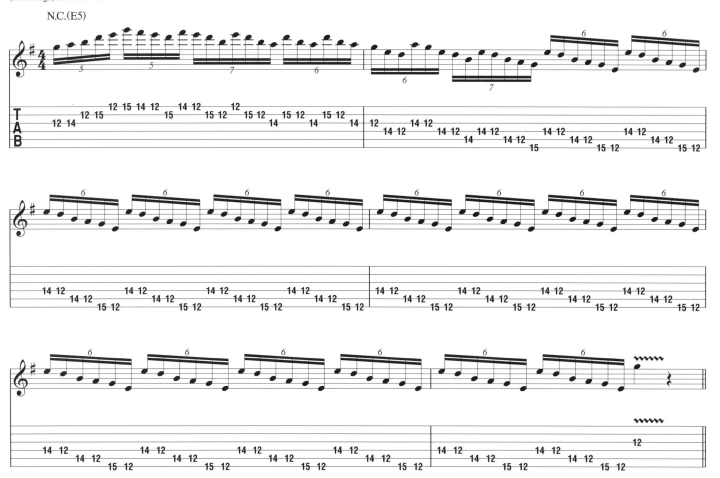

Solo Excerpt #7

The final two examples move further into the solo, and the harmony shifts to an ascending progression that rises from Csus2 to Dsus2 and back to the tonic E5 chord. The first measure occurs at the 9:25 mark and begins with Joe outlining the C chord in the upper octave. Move up in measure 2 to bend the high E string at the 17th and 15th frets with your ring and index fingers, respectively. Bonamassa includes both the raised (natural) and flatted 7ths of the E chord (D# and D) in measure 3, then finishes the line by moving up to 15th position and playing through some jazzy arpeggio shapes that outline the chord nicely. Note the inclusion of both the 9th (F#) and flatted 7th (D) in this measure.

TRACK 39 (Slow demo, 0:12)

Tune down 1 step:
(low to high) D-G-C-F-A-D

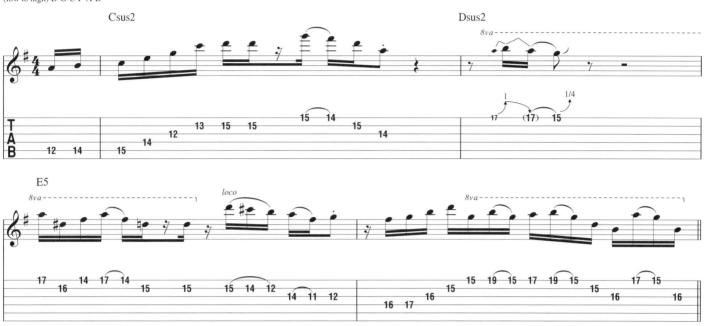

Solo Excerpt #8

The final excerpt from this song starts at 9:33, immediately following the previous example. Begin in 12th position but drop down during the first measure so that the F# on the 11th fret of the G string is played with your index finger, and the 12th-fret notes immediately after are both played with the middle finger. Notice the way Joe superimposes a first inversion A triad (C#-E-A) over the D chord in the second measure before returning to the tried and true E minor pentatonic scale that has made up the bulk of his solo. The phrase ends with a funky, staccato phrase moving between D and B, which he continues in the measures to come as the song works its way towards its conclusion.

TRACK 40 (Slow demo, 0:12)

Tune down 1 step:
(low to high) D-G-C-F-A-D

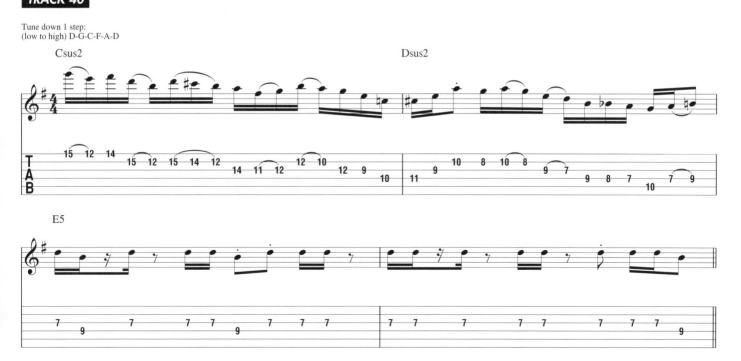

Blues Deluxe

From *Blues Deluxe* (2003)

Words and Music by Rod Stewart and Jeff Beck

Joe's astonishing performance of Rod Stewart's "Blues Deluxe," first recorded by the great Jeff Beck (*Truth*, 1968), is a tour de force of the style. Bonamassa manages to distill the essence of the genre into roughly seven minutes, providing an overview of contemporary, cutting-edge blues guitar, while reflecting the influence of nearly a century's worth of past masters. Bonamassa' playing is both modern, showcasing the latest in technical advancements on the instrument and its tonal possibilities, and classic, demonstrating a tremendous knowledge of the vocabulary and stylistic contributions of earlier generations of practitioners. In short, it merits serious study, so let's take a look at 11 crucial excerpts from this bona fide masterpiece.

Intro Solo, Measures 1-4

Joe begins "Blues Deluxe" with a full 12-bar chorus of soloing, broken down below in three chunks of four measures. Beginning with a familiar melodic motif, he adds the major 3rd (E) to the C minor pentatonic scale during the first two measures, then shifts up to 11th position in measure 3, bending the high E string up a whole step at the 13th fret with his ring finger. Move up again, in measure 4, to perform the 15th-fret bends with your ring finger and the 13th-fret bend with your index finger, unassisted. This is a somewhat difficult maneuver that isn't encountered all that often; you'll need to be both strong and accurate to push the F up to G with a single digit. Joe's old pal B.B. King pulls this one off all the time.

TRACK 41

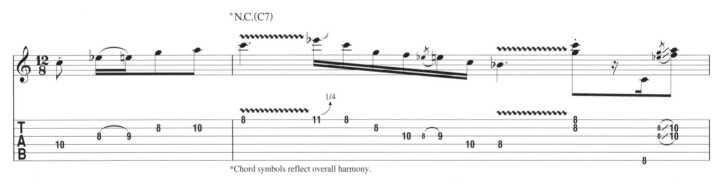

*Chord symbols reflect overall harmony.

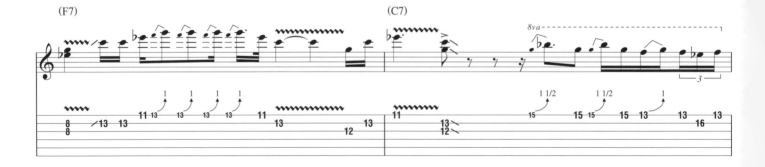

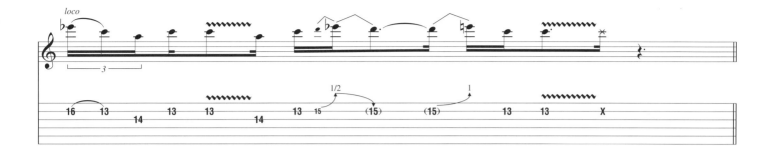

Intro Solo, Measures 5–8

The pickup to the next example finds Joe approaching the IV chord (F7) by way of the C major pentatonic scale, using his index finger to both slide down the D string and inch its way down the A string to the 8th fret as he begins the first measure with an F7 arpeggio. Stay in 8th position here, but use your ring finger to slide up the G string from the 10th to the 11th fret *and* pull-off down to the 8th fret immediately after. The second measure begins with a stinging high C at the 20th fret of the high E string, a drop down for a few 13th-fret bends, then a further shift that puts you in position to perform the remaining 15th-fret bends with your ring finger. That index-finger bend makes another appearance near the end of measure 3 as well.

(Slow demo, 0:27)

TRACK 42

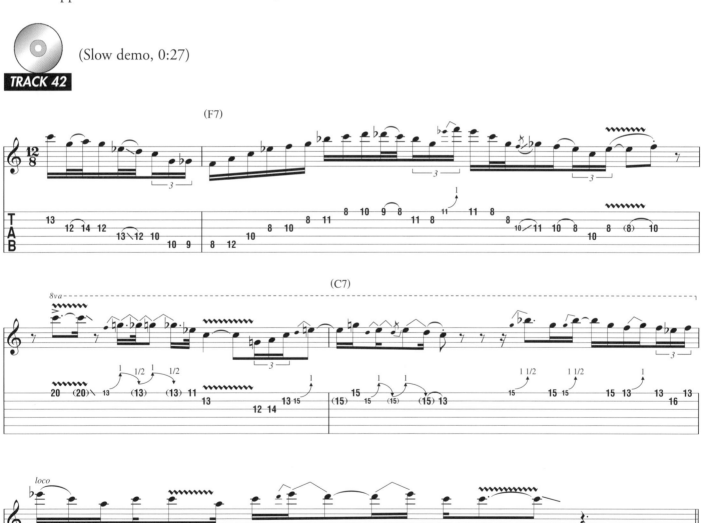

Intro Solo, Measures 9–12

Start the next example in 8th position, with your ring finger handling all the 10th-fret bends on the B and high E strings. The 8th-fret bend in the first measure is another one of those solo index-finger maneuvers, so be sure to raise the string far enough to hit the target D squarely on the nose. The final note in measure 1 should be played with the ring finger, moving you down into 6th position to play over the F7 chord. Bonamassa ends his intro solo with a classic turnaround phrase that should find a welcome home in any blues-guitarist's arsenal.

 (Slow demo, 0:28)

TRACK 43

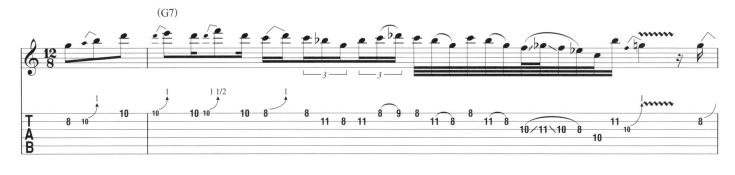

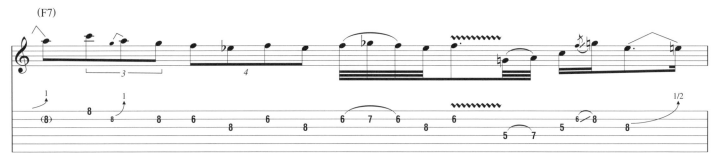

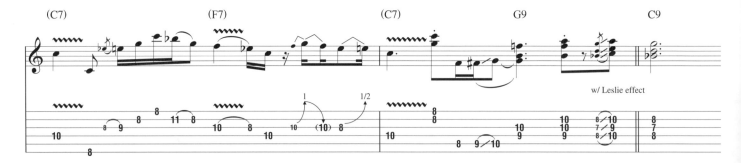

Verse Fill # 1

In the traditional style, Joe fills the gaps between his vocal lines with a series of slashing licks, a call-and-response technique that harkens back to the very beginnings of the blues. This one stays in 8th position for the duration, with each bend taken by the ring finger. Joe mixes notes from both the C major pentatonic and C minor pentatonic scales—another approach that's as old as the style itself—and weaves an intricate rhythmic design that dances across the beat in a particularly complex way. Take the time to learn exactly where each note falls in the measure.

(Slow demo, 0:17)

N.C.(C7)

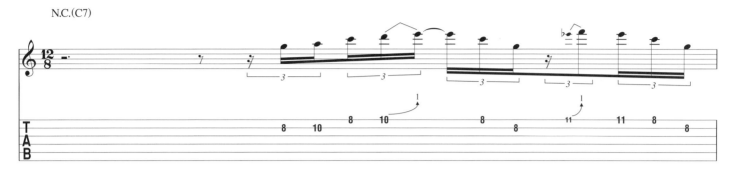

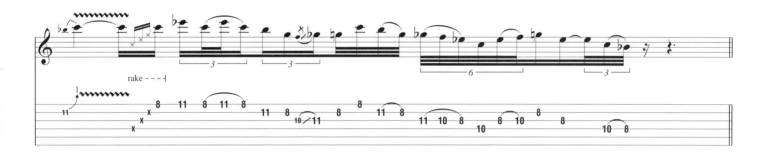

Verse Fill #2

Joe returns below to the melodic motif he introduced in the previous example, bending the 9th (D) up to the major 3rd (E), then bending the minor 3rd (E♭) to the 4th (F) later in the measure. Do your best to hit all three pitches (F, E♭, and E) in this bend accurately—you might want to play each note (on the 13th, 11th, and 12th frets of the high E string, respectively) before attempting the bend to be sure you know exactly how they sound.

(Slow demo, 0:18)

N.C.(C7)

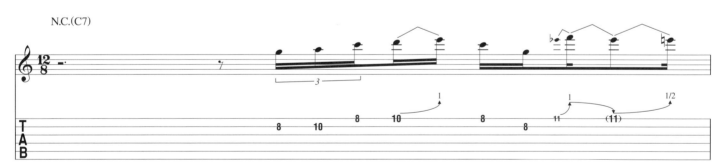

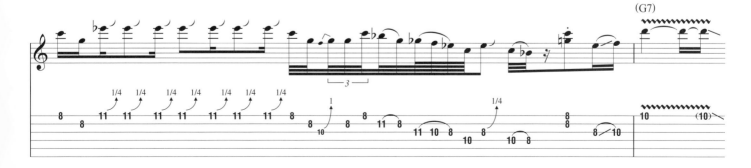

Verse Fill #3

The lick below continues in the razor-sharp rhythmic vein, supplying potent punctuation to Bonamassa's vocals. All bends in the phrase should be played by the ring finger. Stay in the 8th-fret C pentatonic blues box for the duration and extend your pinky to grab the F on the 13th fret of the high E string.

 (Slow demo, 0:13)

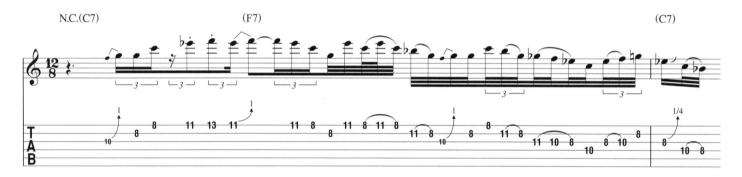

Solo Excerpt #1

We pick up the action as Joe begins his second full solo chorus, giving his volume knob a twist to crank up the overdrive to full blast. Start the phrase by sliding up the G string to the 14th fret with your middle finger, leaving you in 13th position for the duration of the excerpt. End by pushing the B string up a full two whole steps, from E♭ to G, before releasing the bend back down and applying vibrato.

 (Slow demo, 0:17)

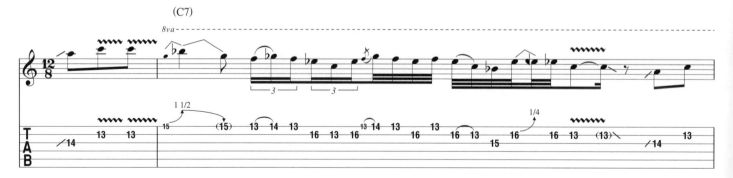

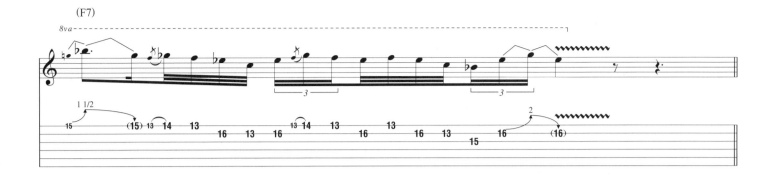

Solo Excerpt #2

The machine-gun spray of the next lick begins immediately after the previous example ends and features a highly repetitive pentatonic idea played primarily in 15th position. Use your ring finger for each 18th-fret bend, including the final one in which both B and high E strings are caught with the same finger. This excerpt isn't too difficult to figure out, but pulling it off at full speed with the correct rhythms is another story. Slow it way down and practice it until you're really nailing those 5- and 6-note groupings precisely. This is truly the modern-day-rock-shredder's side of the blues, a distinct contrast to the old-school sound and phrasing Bonamassa employs earlier in the song.

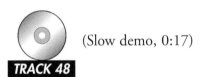

(Slow demo, 0:17)

TRACK 48

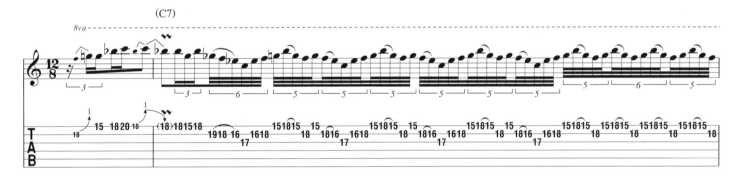

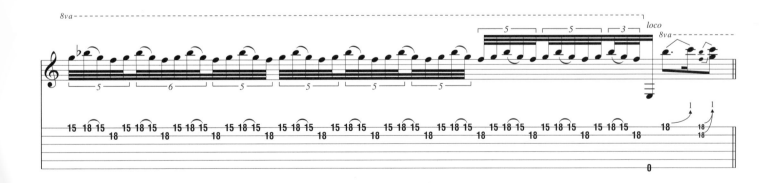

Solo Excerpt #3

Joe keeps the shredfest going as he hits the IV chord (F7), bending both the B and high E strings up a whole step with the ring finger in an unusual five-notes-over-three-beats rhythm, before finishing out the initial measure with a super-fast lick in a somewhat more conventional rhythm. The second measure includes a soaring 20th-fret bend and release on the B string that raises a G up a minor 3rd to Bb.

(Slow demo, 0:17)

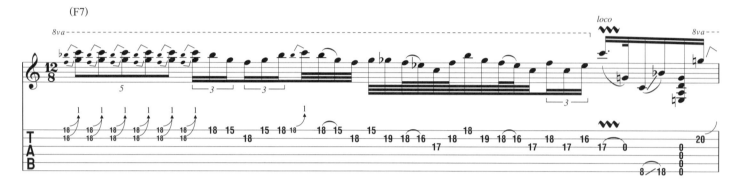

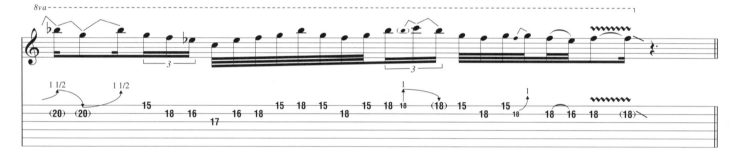

Solo Excerpt #4

This example features a rip-roaring lick played over the V chord (G7). Other then when it slides up the G string from the 10th fret to the 12th fret and back down again, it stays in 8th position throughout. Use your ring finger to slide in both directions, with your middle finger grabbing the Bb on the 11th fret of the B string above.

(Slow demo, 0:13)

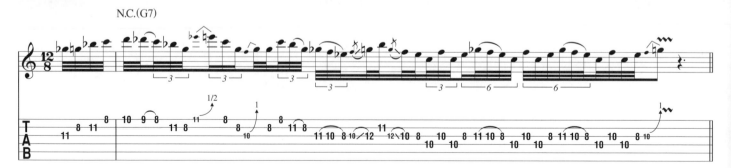

Volume Swell Lick

Joe's violin-like volume swells are decidedly untraditional—you won't hear techniques like this on a B.B. King record—but they're undeniably cool. They're also pretty tricky in that you have to quickly roll the volume up and then back down to (nearly) the off position before each new note is played. Depending on the guitar you're playing, you may have to stretch a fairly long way with your picking hand pinky to manipulate the knob. "Blues Deluxe" was recorded on a Stratocaster, but Joe now plays it on a Les Paul. The latter presents a greater degree of difficulty in reaching the volume knob, particularly because he uses the treble pickup. Interestingly, Bonamassa feels the switch from the Fender to the Gibson has made the song sound much less like Stevie Ray Vaughan. As he notes: "Anybody doing slow-blues playing [on] the fast stuff with the Strat is immediately in that category of being Stevie Ray Vaughan. I am a big of fan of Stevie, but he was not my primary influence." Note the crescendo markings in the second measure—during this part of the phrase, roll the knob back a little bit less for each note so that the level increases and you're at full volume by beat 4, finishing out the lick with a rapid-fire line saturated in distortion.

 (Slow demo, 0:17)

TRACK 51

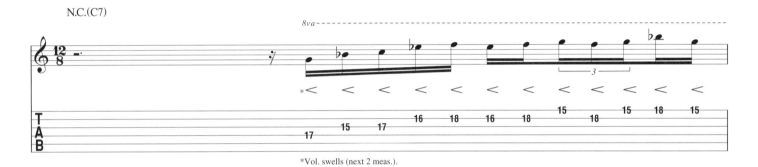

Man of Many Words

From *Blues Deluxe* (2003)

Written by Buddy Guy

Joe Bonamassa is not only a man of many words, but also of many tastes and musical personalities. This solid funk/rock number is actually a cover of an old Buddy Guy classic. Bonamassa gave it an updated arrangement featuring a cushiony organ backdrop, which makes it stand out in sharp contrast to traditional blues numbers like the album's title track and more exploratory songs such as "Pain and Sorrow." It's fun, hip, and straight to the point with short, singable solo sections and a healthy dose of lasciviousness.

Main Riff

This short, simple phrase uses rootless chords and serves as both intro and chorus. Both the C and G7 chords should be played with an index finger barre, with the middle finger hammering-on to the major 3rd of the G7 chord. Don't omit the rhythmic, muted scratch strums that lend the riff such a funky vibe.

TRACK 52

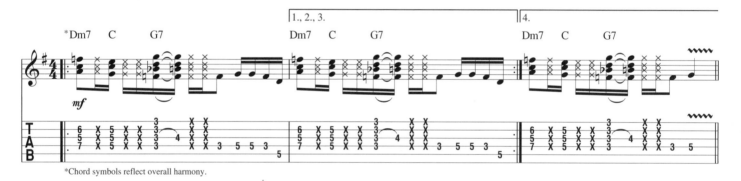

*Chord symbols reflect overall harmony.

Solo I

Joe's first solo—a mere 8 bars—is shown in its entirety below. All the bends in the first two measures should be played with the ring finger, so that you begin in 11th position, but quickly drop down to 8th position at the end of the initial measure. Be sure to push the B string hard enough to raise the B♭ all the way to D in measure 2. There's a tricky little shifting phrase in measure 3 that begins on the E (G string, 9th fret). The slide down the B string should be performed by the index finger, while the G-string slide should be played by the middle finger. Grab the G on the 3rd fret of the high E string with your index finger and then follow up with the G-string slide and pull-off combination. The second half of the solo rises to 15th position and begins with a middle-finger bend on the B string at the 17th fret as Joe combines the G major pentatonic and G minor pentatonic scales. At the end of measure 6, slide up the G string with your middle finger to the 19th fret, grabbing the 20th-fret bend on the high E string with your ring finger, then finish out the solo in the 15th-fret G-pentatonic blues box.

TRACK 53

Solo II, Excerpt #1

Joe's second solo gets a surprising lift from a simple, time-tested arranging trick: changing keys. "It's the old *Star Search* key change," he says, "it always works." The two examples that follow are up a whole step in the key of A. However, the band continues to rise in sections not shown here, all the way to the key of C, before returning to G for the final verse and chorus. This excerpt starts with a middle-finger slide up the G string and some ring-finger bends at the B string's 12th fret. This initial melodic idea becomes a recurring motif throughout the latter parts of the song. Joe moves up quickly—first to 12th position at the end of the opening measure, and then all the way to the 17th-position A-pentatonic fingering near the end of measure 2. There's a cool countrified bend in measure 4, in which the 6th (F#) is raised a half step to G (the flatted 7th) and held while the root (A) is played on the high E string above. Note the inclusion of the major 3rd of the A7 chord (C#) in the line as well, another example of the combination of major and minor pentatonic ideas.

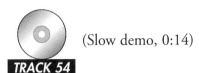 (Slow demo, 0:14)

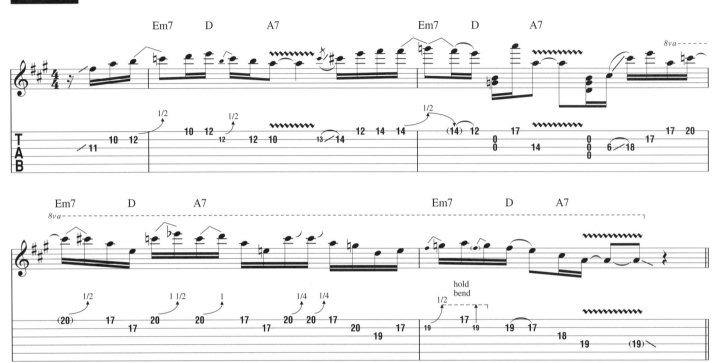

Solo II, Excerpt #2

The last excerpt from this song is a thorny little finger buster. The downward slide on the high E string should be played by your middle finger, which will necessitate using the pinky to play the 17th-fret E's on the B string that follow. The slide up the A string later in the phrase should be played by the ring finger, while the downward G-string slide that ends it should be handled by the index finger. In measure 2, bend the B string at the 17th fret with your ring finger and the G string at the 16th fret with your middle finger. The 13th-fret B-string bend must be taken by the index finger. The whole lick is not only difficult to play but rhythmically complex as well—take your time with this one.

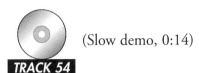 (Slow demo, 0:09)

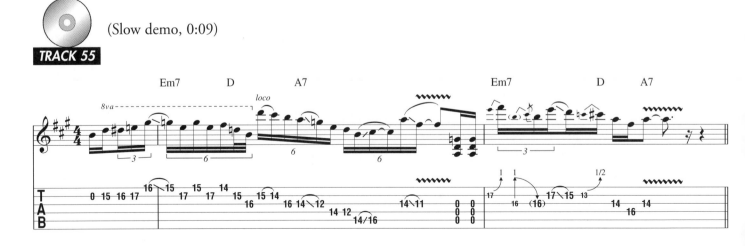

Revenge of the 10 Gallon Hat

From *Had to Cry Today* (2004)

Words and Music by Joe Bonamassa

As a kid, Joe was a close friend and protégé of the late, great Telecaster-master Danny Gatton. "Revenge of the 10 Gallon Hat" is Joe's tribute to his mentor, a man who not only encouraged him and filled with him with confidence, but also helped shape his musical sensibilities by directing him towards the work of such diverse players as Scotty Moore, Duane Eddy, Chuck Berry, Merle Travis, Wes Montgomery, and others. This song was written on Bonamassa's 1954 Fender Esquire (a rare gem) and is played with a capo on the 2nd fret. You can play the song without the capo, but you won't be able to play along with the recording unless you are a fan of some pretty strange harmonies. Note that all pitches are shown in the notation as if they were played *sans* capo. The fret numbers in the tablature follow the same principle; a 0 on the low E string will sound like an F♯ but will still be played without using your left hand. "10 Gallon Hat" is pretty quick; take your time working the licks up to speed so that they're clean, crisp, and just as pretty as Joe makes them. Also, notice Joe's extensive use of chromatic *connector* notes in the licks below. They're never used haphazardly, but instead occur at precise points in the line, and are highly specific stylistic devices common to both country and jazz.

Intro Riff

This recurring riff is played in 1st position, so that all 2nd-fret notes are played by the middle finger, including the barred double-stop in measure 8. The hammer-on to the major 3rd (G♯) that follows should be played by the index finger.

(Slow demo, 0:17)

Riff II

During the first twelve measures of this descending progression, use a parallel fingering scheme as you work your way down the neck: your ring finger will play both the D-string notes and the barred double-stops on the G and B strings, while your index barres the high E and B strings, and your middle finger performs the G-string hammer-ons to the major 3rds of each chord in the progression (E, D, A, G, F♯, and F). The phrase ends with a flashy pull-off lick that moves from the 3rd and 2nd frets to each open string, ultimately leading back to the opening riff illustrated in the previous example.

(Slow demo, 0:16)

TRACK 57

Solo Excerpt #1

The difficult lick below occurs at the 1:14 mark of the recording (approximately). The speed of the line makes for a real challenge, and the fingering must be handled with care, as well. Begin by sliding up the A string with your ring finger, then slide down the G string with your index finger. As you descend in diatonic 6ths, the index finger will continue to handle all G-string notes, while those on the A string must be taken by the middle or ring fingers, depending on whether they are one or two frets above the G-string note they follow. Drop to 1st position in measure 3, using your middle finger for the 2nd-fret notes. Check out the cool octave idea in the final measure, in which the open high E string is followed by a slide into the E at the D string's 14th fret and 3 quick strikes of the open low E string below. Pretty slick!

(Slow demo, 0:05)

TRACK 58

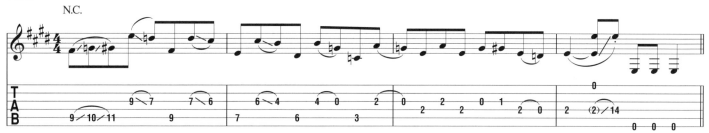

Solo Excerpt #2

The next lick, hot on the heels of the previous example, is one long string of eighth notes running seven full measures before finally coming to rest at the open low E string on the downbeat of measure 8. Start with a *pitch-matching* bend, in which the ring finger pushes the D at the B string's 15th-fret up a whole step to match the E played by the index finger above. After releasing the bend, begin the descent with your index finger taking all the notes on the high E string, and your middle and ring fingers playing the B-string notes below. There's some quick shifting ahead: pull off from the 5th fret to the 3rd fret and open high E string with your ring and index fingers, then begin measure 4 in 4th position as you climb chromatically from the major 3rd (G♯) to the (B). Drop down on the final beat of the measure to play the D with your middle finger and the F♯ with your index finger—a very brisk fingering transition. From measure 6 to the end of the phrase, remain in 1st position, with your middle finger taking all the notes on the second fret, in addition to the low-E-string bend and release.

(Slow demo, 0:09)

TRACK 59

Solo Excerpt #3

The 16-measure excerpt below immediately follows the last lick and begins in 5th position, with a hammer-on from the index finger to the ring finger on the A string. Stay in this position until measure 3, where you'll need to slide down the D string with your index finger and perform pull-offs to the open string as well. Shift quickly in measure 4 so that your index finger slides up the A string and performs the pull-off as well. At the end of measure 5, hammer-on from your middle finger to your ring finger, putting yourself in 1st position until you slide up the B string with your ring finger at the end of measure 8. Play the repeated phrase in measures 9, 10, and 11 in 3rd position, and then return to 1st position on beat 2 of measure 12 (the A on the G string's 2nd fret, played by the middle finger). Finish the excerpt without shifting again—those low-E-string bends in the final measures should be played by the middle finger as well.

 (Slow demo, 0:16)

TRACK 60

Solo Excerpt #4

Let's take a look at one more super-cool, chicken-pickin' lick before we finish with "10 Gallon Hat." This excerpt occurs immediately after the previous example, when the harmony moves up to the IV. The bass pedals on an A while the rhythm guitar lays down a series of triads (A, G, D) and an A7 chord. Start in 2nd position, with your index finger handling all the 2nd-fret notes and pull-offs, and then slide up the G string with your middle finger at the end of measure 2. In measure 3, play the 5th-fret A on the high E string with your ring finger and remain in this position until you drop down a fret for the final note of measure 4 (a D♯ played by the ring finger). You're now in 2nd position, where you should remain for the rest of the excerpt. Grab the A on the high E string in measure 5 with your pinky. In measure 7, perform the 3rd- and 2nd-fret A-string bends with your middle and ring fingers, respectively, pulling towards the floor.

 (Slow demo, 0:09)

Capo II

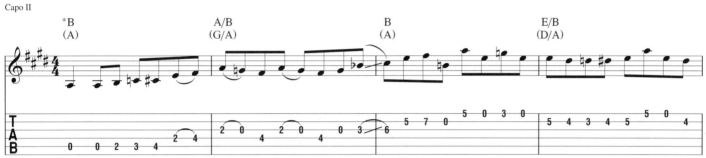

*Symbols in parentheses represent chord names respective to capoed guitars.
Symbols above reflect actual sounding chords. Capoed fret is "0" in tab.

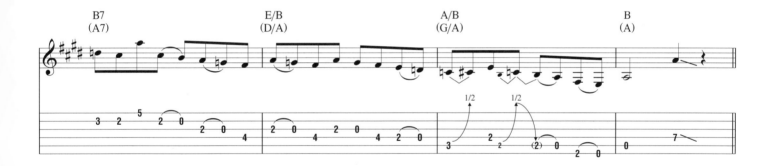

The River

From *Had to Cry Today* (2004)

By Joe Bonamassa and Bob Held

TRACK 62

Tuning track (Open E tuning, up 1/2 step;
low to high: F-C-F-A-C-F)

Inspired by the Delta blues classic "When the Levee Breaks" and by an old Mississippi Fred McDowell performance (*Live at Newport 1964*), "The River" was recorded on both electric guitar and on a 1931 National steel-bodied resonator. Both instruments are tuned to open F (F-C-F-A-C-F, low to high). As Joe says: "Tuning your guitar from open E to open F creates a hotter tone. It's a little more vibrant, has a little more vitality." It's also an easier and more vibrant key for him to sing in. "The River" takes us on a highly evocative, multifaceted musical journey, full of rich textures, dark and soulful acoustic playing, and heavily distorted electric slide work that brings to mind Led Zeppelin's classic 1971 version of "When the Levee Breaks."

Dobro Lick #1

You don't need a steel guitar to play the intro licks below, although you will get a more authentic tone if you use one. The free-time or *rubato* nature of the phrases make the rhythms on the page something of an approximation; listen closely to the recording to capture the spirit and flow of these lines. Joe returns to the opening idea a handful of times, with subtle variation, throughout the acoustic intro section. Use your index finger for the G-string slides and your ring finger for the 3rd-fret notes that follow.

TRACK 63

Open E tuning, up 1/2 step:
(low to high) F-C-F-A-C-F

Dobro Lick #2

The next lick serves as an answer to Joe's vocal lamentations ("Where I could just lay down and die"). It's fairly simple; play it in 1st position, with your ring finger taking all 3rd-fret notes and the A-string slide up to the 5th fret. The challenge here is all in the attitude and the emotion—it's not just a string of notes, it's a mournful cry, full of pain and regret. Speak through your instrument and bring these feelings to life. That's what the blues is *really* all about—not just shredding your way through pentatonic scales.

Open E tuning, up 1/2 step:
(low to high) F-C-F-A-C-F

N.C.

Electric Intro Riff

Now we really crank things up with the entrance of the full band, saturated electric guitar tone, and wailing har-monica a la Robert Plant. Throughout the riff below, Joe alternates between standard fretting and slide techniques, with a metal or brass slide worn on the ring finger. If you're new to slide guitar, you will likely need to do a bit of remedial study and a good deal of practice before you're able to pull off this kind of playing cleanly. While the sub-ject is broad enough to deserve its own book—and there are numerous fine publications available on the subject—here are some general pointers that will make your life easier. First, dampening is crucial. Both hands must carefully mute unused strings to avoid excessive noise and whining. Flatten your index finger (and possibly your middle fin-ger as well) on the strings behind the slide as you move up and down the neck. The side of your right hand and indi-vidual fingers can also be used to control the noise. An experienced slide guitarist playing a lick on the G string, for example, will often pluck with his or her index finger while using the thumb to dampen the D string below and the middle and ring fingers to mute the open B and high E strings above. Experiment with dampening techniques to make your slide playing quieter and more controlled.

Next, realize that slide playing is much easier on a guitar with relatively high action. As the slide must be laid gently on the string, above the fret metal (rather than over the wood), excessively low action will result in a lot of clanking and choked notes as the result of coming into contact with the actual fret. The old school resonators were often set up with strings so high that they were nearly impossible to play *without* a slide. You don't have to go that far, but a happy medium between super-high action and ultra-low shred-style string height should yield good results.

Finally, understand that just because it's called "slide" does not mean you have to slide into every note, and that even when you do it doesn't have to be from a long distance or in an exaggerated way, which will ultimately wind up sounding pretty silly. Joe's slides are usually very controlled, with the wild plunging and gliding effects held in reserve for added impact when necessary. In the excerpt below, any slides up or down that do not have a specifically notat-ed end point should travel only a few frets at most. Vibrato, applied by rapidly shaking the slide from left to right a *short* distance, should likewise by contained so that the desired effect is creating without the actual pitches being pulled severely out of tune. Precise intonation is the hallmark of a skilled slide guitarist and often the last element of the style to solidify; practice carefully and hit your marks without sliding past the notes or falling short.

TRACK 65

Open E tuning, up 1/2 step:
(low to high) F-C-F-A-C-F

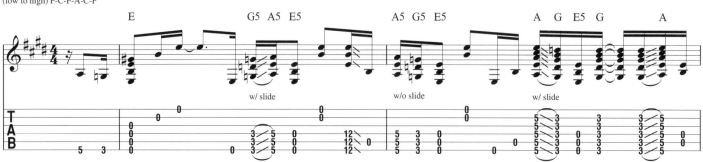

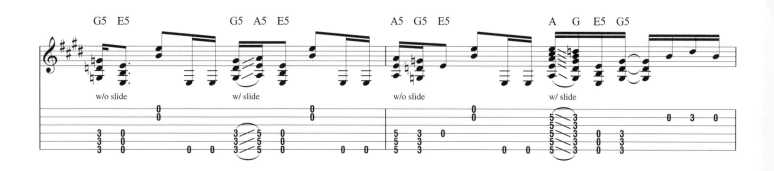

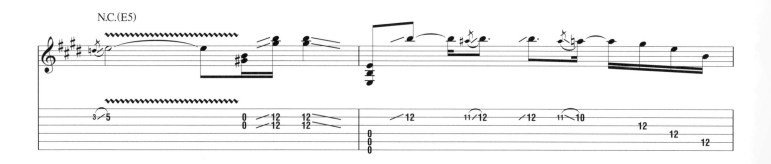

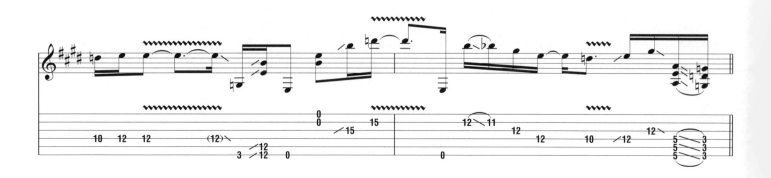

Chorus Excerpt

This richly ringing phrase echoes the descending sequence first heard in the acoustic introduction. It's quite easy to play, but I'd suggest doing so while wearing the slide on your ring finger, the way Joe does, to get used to playing standard fretted ideas while encumbered by the bottleneck.

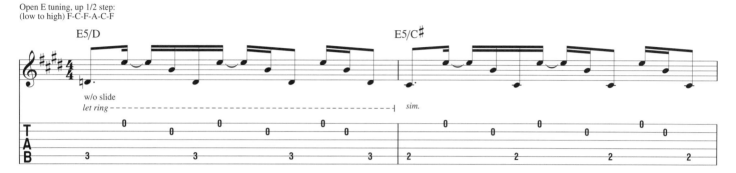

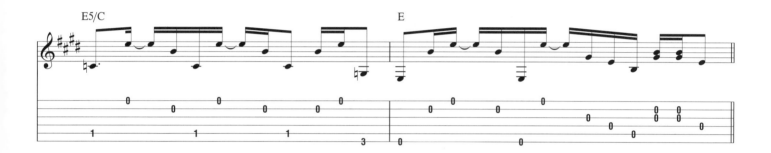

Solo

Let's take a look at Joe's full eight-measure slide solo. Begin by sliding up to the 12th fret from a fret or two below and play the first 10th-fret grouping by lifting the slide away from the neck and fretting these notes normally. Be careful not to bring the slide down too heavily on beat 3 of the measure as you slide back up. You'll have amply opportunity to practice this technique in measures 3 (the D on beat 4) and 4 (the 3rd-fret notes beginning on beat 2). In both cases, the notes must be played by the slide—*without sliding*. Merely lay it down softly, right above the fret metal, without pushing down into the strings. During the high-register 16th-note licks in measures 6 and 7, only slide audibly from chord to chord where indicated; otherwise simply move the slide from fret to fret while muting carefully so that the notes are discretely separated. Bonamassa employs another cool technique in the final measure, when he picks four-note groupings on the A and low E strings once each and uses the slide to pull-off to the open string. It's a bit tricky in that you have to lift off with enough force to sound the open string without hitting any other strings or making a lot of unwanted noise. Now would be a good time to put those picking hand dampening techniques to use: try laying your middle fingertip on the D string when pulling off to the open A string, then repeat the procedure with the A string when you pull off to open E.

(Slow demo, 0:31)

TRACK 67

Open E tuning, up 1/2 step:
(low to high) F-C-F-A-C-F

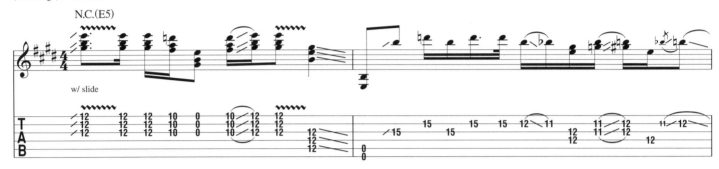

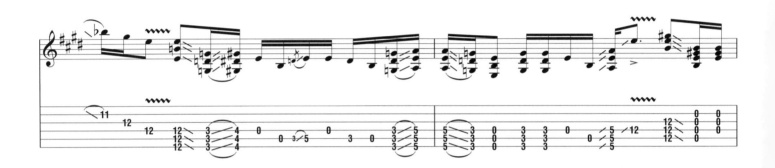

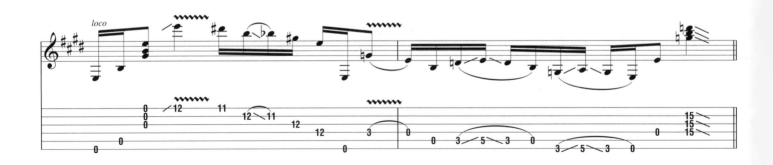

Bridge to Better Days

From *You & Me* (2006)

Words and Music by Joe Bonamassa

This foot-stomping number from Bonamassa's fifth studio album reveals the heavy influence of British blues, melding hard-edged guitar tones, syncopated funk rhythms, and unmistakable blues underpinnings in both its structure and melodic components. It's also a testament to Joe's evolving, ever-maturing songwriting style, with a stripped-down vibe that leaves only the essential elements: strong vocal hooks, memorable riffs, and room for yet another classic solo.

Intro Riff

The intro to "Bridge to Better Days" is such a strong piece of multi-guitar arranging that it is shown in its entirety below, with Guitar 1 on the bottom staff, Guitar 2 in slashes above, and Guitar 3, the lead line, on the top staff. Note the 12-bar structure of this section and of the opening verse; this is an updated blues, with untraditional harmonies and grooves, but it's a blues nonetheless. Let's take a closer look at each guitar part, beginning with guitar 1, which brings the funk via a 16th-note double-stop riff. After the initial low-E-string notes, jump up quickly to play the E and G with your middle and index fingers on the G and B strings, respectively. In measures 5 and 6, when the chord shifts to the IV in 1st inversion (D with an F♯ in the bass), the D7 shape on the top three strings is played first in the lower register and then raised an octave. The turnaround progression begins on the ♭VI chord (Fadd9), with the thumb taking the root on the low E string, the index finger on the B string, ring finger on the D string, and middle finger performing the G-string pull-off. In measure 10, we rise from the V (E) to the ♭VII (G) before returning to the original double-stop idea.

Guitar 2 (in slashes for the first nine measures) has a simpler part, with power chords on the lower two strings, as well as the inverted roots and 3rds of the C/E and D/F♯ chords. The inversions continue in measure 10, where the E and G chords are played in 3-note voicings with the 3rds on the D string, 5ths on the G string, and roots on the B string above. Guitar 3 layers solo licks on top, entering at the end of measure 2 with a pre-bend on the G string. This means you will have to bend the D up a whole step to E *before* striking the note, releasing it, and pushing it back up. This can be a bit tricky at first, as you have to know exactly how far to push the string to hit the targeted pitch accurately. At the end of measure 4, slide up the D string with your ring finger, then use the same finger for the B-string bend. The A on the 17th fret of the high E string must be grabbed by the pinky. In measure 6, play the 14th-fret, sliding double stops with your ring finger and the combinations on the G and B strings with your index and middle fingers, respectively. The double-bend in the following measure should be played with your ring finger bending both B and high E strings simultaneously. During the ringing turnaround phrase in measures 9 and 10, your middle finger will take all D-string notes while your ring finger gets to the B-string notes above.

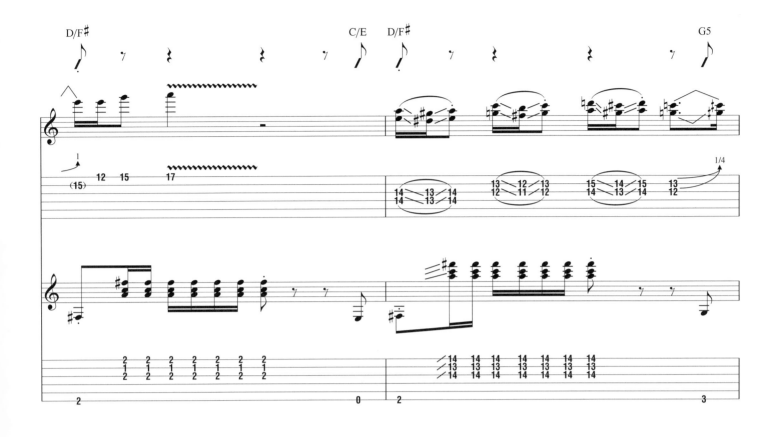

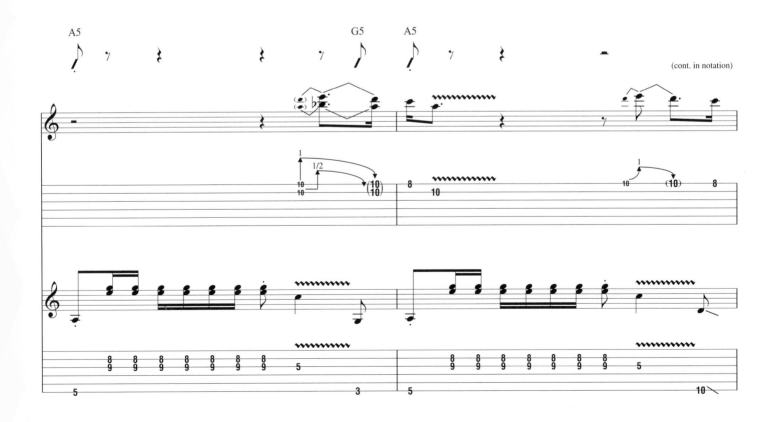

(cont. in notation)

Pre-Solo Riff

This short phrase is played twice and serves as a kind of send-off that launches Joe into his solo. Begin in 5th position with your index finger barring the top three strings as indicated in the first measure, then play the sliding double-stops in measure 2 with your index and middle fingers on the D and B strings. The riff ends with ascending power chords that rise from F♯ back up to the tonic (A).

TRACK 69

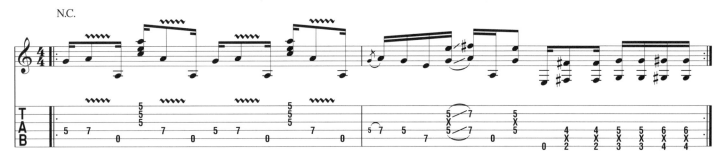

Solo Excerpt #1

"Bridge to Better Days" features two solos played back to back, with distinctly different guitar sounds employed over two different chord progressions. Let's take a look at the complete first solo, running 24 measures in total, divided into three separate 8-measure sections. Joe begins with a rake across the top four strings with his Vox wah pedal in full effect, as the rhythm section continues to play the pre-solo riff (from the previous example). Aside from the quick slides in measure 2, he remains in 5th position throughout the opening four measures, playing from the A minor pentatonic scale with the added 6th degree (F♯). As the band moves up to the IV (D), Joe shifts up as well, repeatedly bending the G string at the 10th fret up a half step to F♯ (the major 3rd of the chord) while grabbing the G (the 4th) with his index finger on the B string above. He climbs again at the end of measure 6, bending the high E with his index finger, and then uses his ring finger for the 10th-fret bends. The excerpt ends where it began, returning to the 5th-fret blues-box fingering.

(Slow demo, 0:27)
TRACK 70

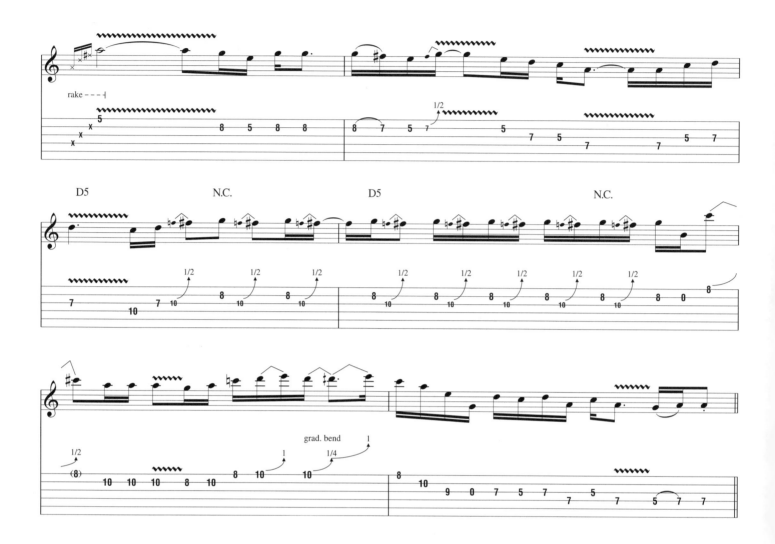

Solo Excerpt #2

Joe really steps up the intensity in the next eight measures, making a quick leap up to 17th position for some A pentatonic licks in the higher register. Use your ring finger for all the bends, including the held 17th-fret B-string bend at the end of measure 2, and the 16th-fret G-string bend at the end of measure 3. While holding the latter, use your right-hand index finger to tap the string at the 20th fret. At the same time, sweep across the frequency spectrum slowly with the wah pedal to create an insane, kaleidoscopic effect. The excerpt ends with a drop back down to the 5th-position A minor pentatonic scale and another lightning fast, wildly wailing phrase.

(Slow demo, 0:27)

TRACK 71

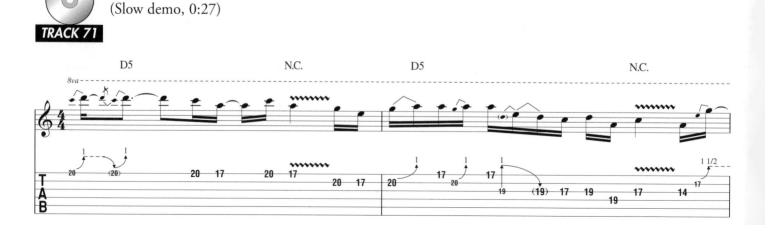

Solo Excerpt #3

Speed and intensity remain at fever pitch during the final segment of the solo, played over a progression that descends twice from E, then rises from A to D twice in its second half. The shifting chords are used primarily for root movement, creating harmonic interest and tension behind Joe's licks. During the first four measures, he plays from the E minor pentatonic scale, with the 6th (C♯) and 9th (F♯) lending the lines additional color and melodic interest. Measures 5 through 8 find Joe returning to the A minor pentatonic scale in the upper octave (17th position). There's nothing particularly odd in terms of techniques or fingerings in this segment, but look out: some of these licks are fast and are likely to put a heavy strain on the chops of even the most skilled players. The 32nd-note line in measure 3, for instance, is particularly tough. Take your time building them up to speed, and don't be discouraged if it doesn't happen overnight. This level of virtuoso playing is extremely difficult to achieve. Most players will never reach this rarefied air, but all will be better for having made the effort.

(Slow demo, 0:27)

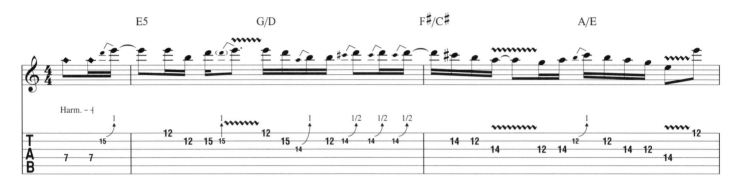

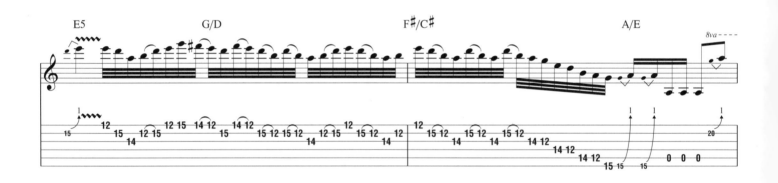

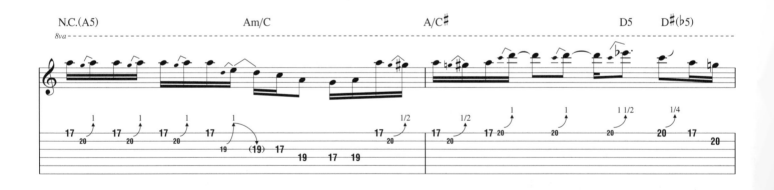

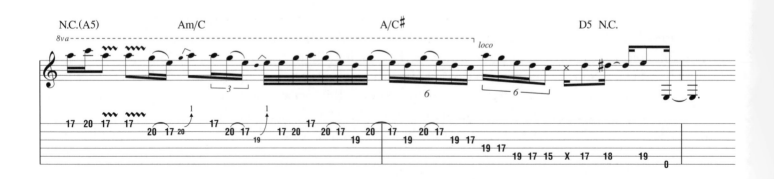

So Many Roads, So Many Trains

From *You & Me* (2006)

Paul Marshall's "So Many Roads," a staple number for both John Mayall and Otis Rush, is a slowly smoldering minor blues in much the same mold as Warren Haynes' "If Heartaches Were Nickels." The key of F minor is a strong one for Joe's voice, and he delivers a confident, impassioned performance, with plenty of fiery solo lines that travel the neck from the 1st-position F minor pentatonic blues box to the same fingering in the upper octave (13th fret) and a variety of mid-fretboard scale positions, as well. Joe has always moved between both vertical (single-position scale playing) and horizontal (multi-position) playing with ease, and the excerpts below demonstrate his methods for moving up and down the neck freely. Study them closely and break out of the blues scale box for good!

Intro Solo, Measures 1–4

"So Many Roads" begins with a full 12-bar solo, examined below in three separate four-measure excerpts. Joe starts in 4th position playing the 6th-fret B-string F and the high-E-string bends in measures 2 and 3 with his ring finger. In the final measure, he moves up the neck into the 13th-fret fingering of the F minor pentatonic scale for a tasty little flurry of notes.

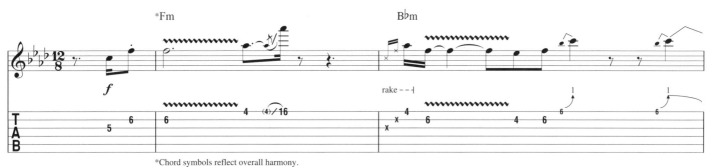

*Chord symbols reflect overall harmony.

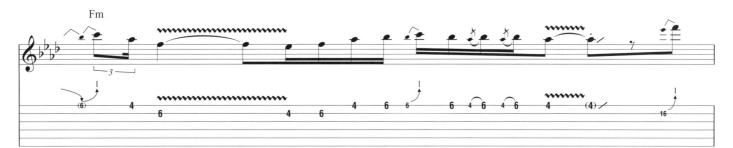

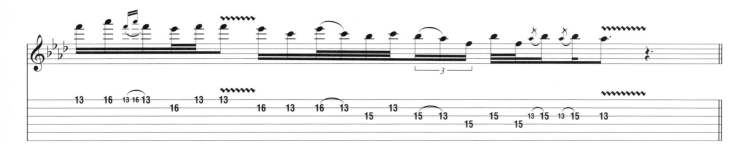

Intro Solo, Measures 5-8

The next excerpt shows off Bonamassa's mobility and knowledge of the fretboard, with an opening phrase in 13th position, a shift down in measure 2 to bend the B string with the ring finger at the 13th fret, and a return to both the 1st-position pentatonic box and 4th-position F minor fingering that the solo began with. The bends in measure 2 are a bit tricky in that you must first overbend the B string up a minor 3rd from C to E♭, then bend both the 12th-fret B and 11th-fret B♭ up to C in quick succession—with the same (middle) finger.

TRACK 74

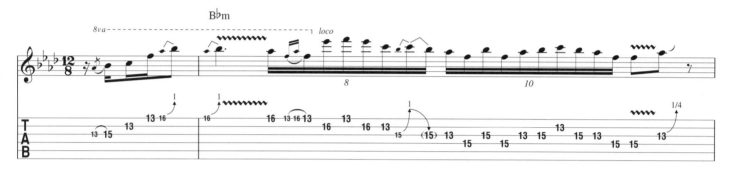

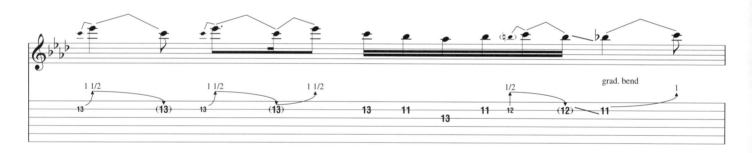

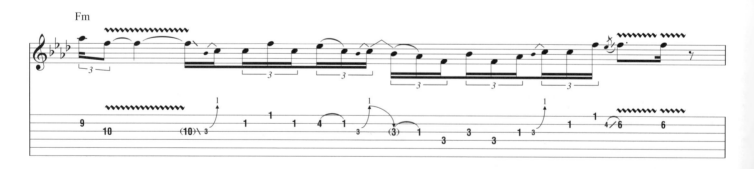

Intro Solo, Measures 9-12

Joe starts the turnaround portion of the chorus with two quick grace-note hammer-ons on the G string, then bends the B string with his ring finger, grabbing the 11th-fret E♭ on the high E string above with his pinky. It's yet another F minor fingering (the fourth distinctly different fingering employed so far), with the tonic located on the G string's 10th fret. Joe supplements the pentatonic sound with a D♭, the minor 3rd of the B♭ minor chord, in measure 2 of the example. The solo ends with a rising octave riff that punctuates each chorus of the song. Use your index finger on the low E string, flattened slightly to mute the unused A string, and your ring finger on the D string for each of the octave groupings.

TRACK 75

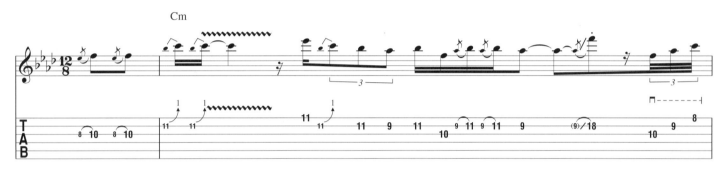

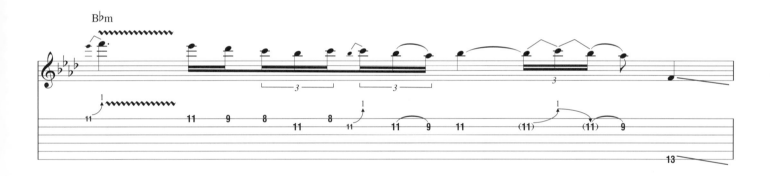

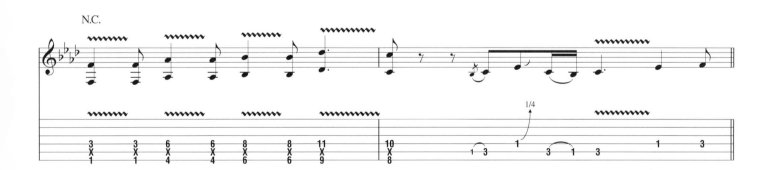

Solo Excerpt #1

Joe's next solo, which follows the second verse, starts with repeated unison bends in which the ring finger pushes the B string up a whole step to match the F played on the high E string above. He follows with a string of quick pentatonic lines played strictly in 13th position. Do your best to play the rhythms accurately; the groups of 11 and 10 over 3 beats each are unusual and challenging, to say the least.

(Slow demo, 0:17)

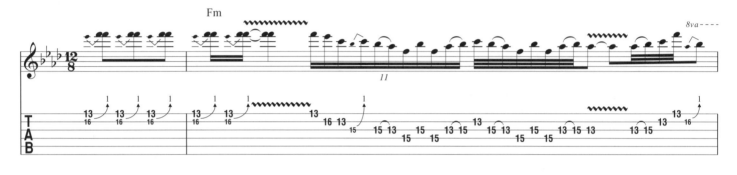

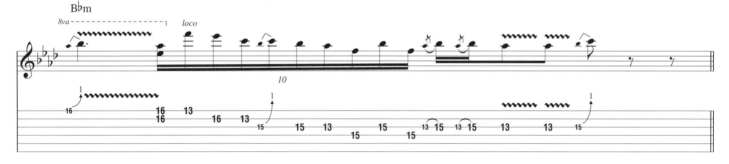

Solo Excerpt #2

The next example coincides with the arrival of the iv chord (B♭ minor, measure 5 of the solo) and also remains in the 13th-position F minor pentatonic scale fingering. After the initial 16th-fret bend, play the F on the high E string's 13th fret with your index finger, then roll down to grab the 13th-fret C on the B string with the same finger—don't lift your hand away from the strings at all during this process.

(Slow demo, 0:13)

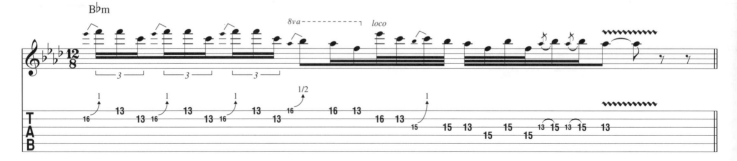

Verse Fill

Here's a particularly tasty fill Bonamassa plays in answer to his vocal in the third verse. We begin in 13th position but extend to grab the 20th-fret C with the pinky, then bend the high E string at the 18th fret with the ring finger. Towards the end of the opening measure, Joe adds the 9th of the Fm chord (G) to the line and then descends the neck in a flurry of pentatonic combinations. The grace note slide down the A string near the end of the phrase should be played with your ring finger, shifting you quickly into 11th position to end the excerpt.

(Slow demo, 0:17)

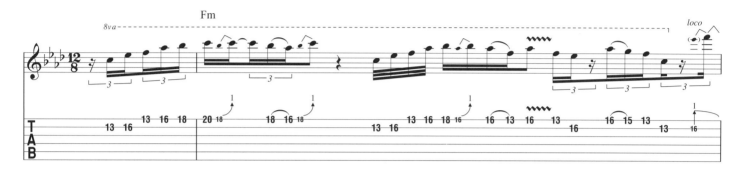

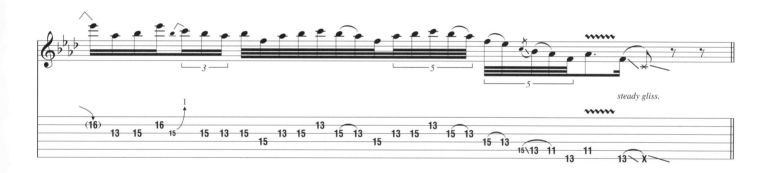

Solo II, Excerpt #1

Joe's third full solo chorus begins with another lightning-fast F pentatonic lick in 13th position. Stay strictly in this fingering except during the ring finger, G-string slide in the first measure that (very) temporarily climbs to the 17th fret. Once again, the crucial aspect of the phrase is rhythm, with tricky ten- and five-note groupings, as well as blisteringly fast 32nd-note runs that will likely send even those with exceptional technique running off to the shed for a bit of an alternate picking workout.

(Slow demo, 0:17)

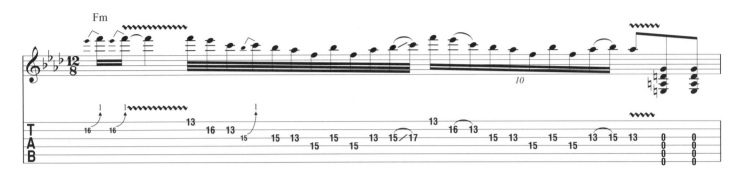

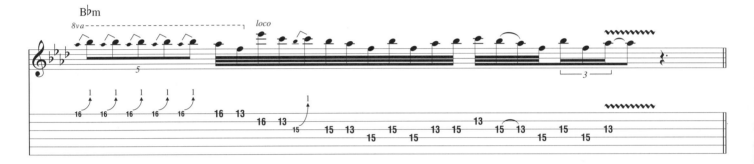

Solo II, Excerpt #2

The next lick is played over the iv chord, later in the same chorus as the previous example. Begin in 16th position, bending the high E string at the 18th fret with your ring finger, then shift down to perform the 16th-fret bends with your middle finger. Halfway through the opening measure, you will be back in the 13th-fret F pentatonic fingering, where you'll finish out the phrase. In measure 2, use your ring finger to bend both B and high E strings simultaneously, with a full two whole steps (major 3rd) bend near the end of the excerpt. Push them strings baby!

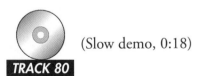

(Slow demo, 0:18)

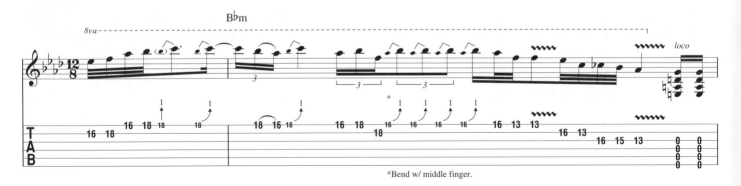

*Bend w/ middle finger.

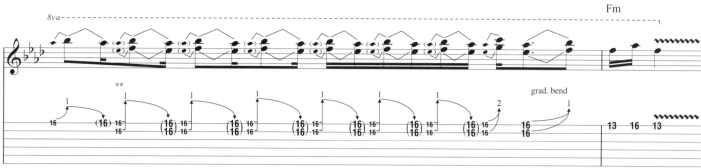

**Catch and bend both strings w/ ring finger.

Solo II, Excerpt #3

Our final excerpt from this song is played over the v-iv (Cm-B♭m) turnaround. This one begins in 11th position, with the ring finger overbending the B string at the 13th fret, raising the C all the way to E♭. At the end of the measure, move up to 13th position and play the 16th- and 15th-fret bends that follow with your ring finger. Note that the B- and G-string bends in the beginning of measure 2 are pre-bends, meaning that the strings will have to be raised to the indicated pitches (F and C, respectively) before you pick and release them back down (you shouldn't hear either string being raised at all). At the end of the measure, Joe drops all the way down the neck to be in position for the octave riff that occurs there and at the end of each chorus.

(Slow demo, 0:18)

TRACK 81

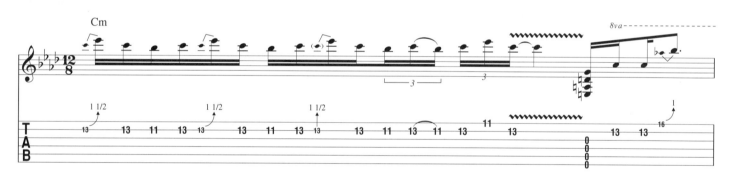

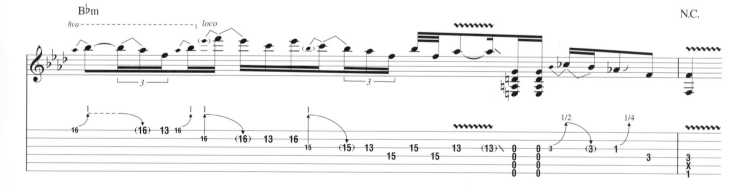

Dirt in My Pocket

From *Sloe Gin* (2007)

Words and Music by Joe Bonamassa and Jim Huff

Tuning track (Open E tuning; low to high: E-B-E-G♯-B-E)

TRACK 82

With a wide variety of textures and sounds, "Dirt in My Pocket" represents another step in Joe Bonamassa's evolution as a guitarist, singer, and songwriter. The dramatic dynamic shifts, open-E tuning electric-slide work, and droning acoustic guitars create a vivid orchestration for this highly focused, streamlined composition. It's not that Joe has abandoned the knockout, extended solos for good; rather, his increased emphasis on memorable songs and musical storytelling has added a new and highly intriguing facet to his already impressive vision. "Dirt in My Pocket" is a relatively easy song from a guitarist's standpoint, but that's beside the point—it packs an unadulterated punch of raw, emotional intensity.

Intro Riff

Joe layers four guitars to create the simple-but-massive sounding riff below. Guitars 1 and 2 play identical parts, although Guitar 1 is a 12-string acoustic and Guitar 2 is a standard electric. The open-E tuning allows for barred power chord shapes on the low E and A strings. Guitars 3 and 4 are both electrics played with slide, although their parts are separated by an octave, with the latter relegated to the high E string while the former stays primarily on the D string throughout the excerpt.

TRACK 83

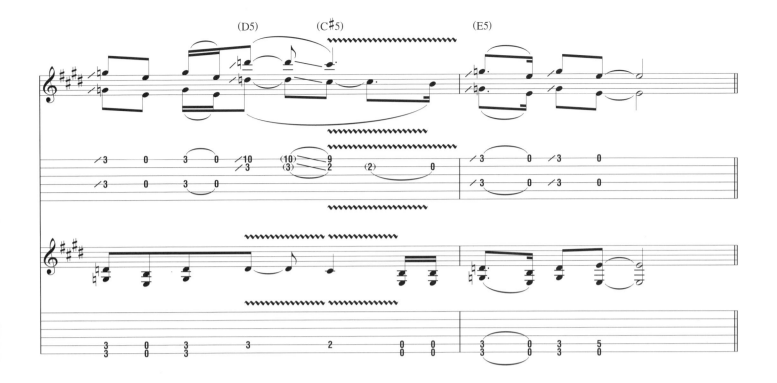

Verse Riff

The verse accompaniment is paired down to a single 12-string acoustic guitar, contrasting nicely with the powerful wall of sound that both precedes and follows it. This easy riff could, of course, be played on any conventional guitar if you don't own or have access to a 12-string. Pick carefully as you jump from string to string and be sure to get enough arch on your left-hand fingers to allow all the notes to ring freely. This one should sound rich and resonant regardless of the guitar you choose to play it on.

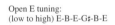

Open E tuning:
(low to high) E-B-E-G♯-B-E

Instrumental Interlude

This short 12-string passage, later augmented by sustained electric guitars, has a quasi-Indian, almost raga-like flavor due in large part to its droning high E string and E Mixolydian (E-F#-G#-A-B-C#-D) modality (the funky tabla groove laid down by keyboardist Rick Melick doesn't hurt either). In the final measure, the mode shifts briefly to E Ionian (the basic E major scale) with the inclusion of the D#. The mixing of modes over a single root note is also commonly encountered in the sarod- and sitar-driven ragas improvised by the masters of Indian classical styles.

 (Slow demo, 0:16)

TRACK 85

Open E tuning:
(low to high) E-B-E-G#-B-E

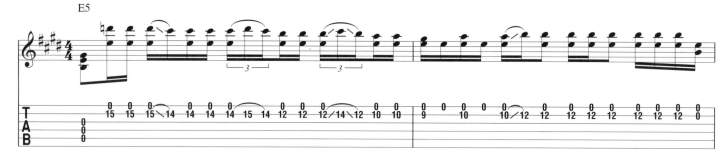

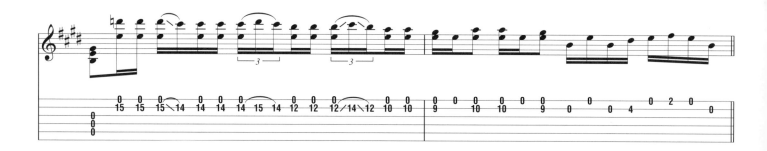

The Ballad of John Henry

From *The Ballad of John Henry* (2009)

Words and Music by Joe Bonamassa

Tuning track (Tune down 2 1/2 steps;
low to high: B-E-A-D-F♯-B)

The final song in our exploration of the music of Joe Bonamassa is the title track of his seventh studio album, a fascinating piece of work that conjures entire worlds of sound and imagery. Combining powerful vocals and vivid storytelling with a diverse palette of guitar tones and timbres, "The Ballad of John Henry" is truly a masterwork of conception, performance, and recording techniques.

Joe recorded the song on an Ernie Ball/Music Man John Petrucci baritone guitar, which is tuned down a perfect 4th (B-E-A-D-F♯-B), presenting a bit of a conundrum for those of us who don't own such an instrument—meaning, nearly all of us. You have a few choices: 1) go out and buy one, 2) tune your standard guitar all the way down to B, or 3) simply play the song as notated in standard tuning. Tuning down may be problematic because your strings will be exceedingly floppy at such a highly reduced level of tension, and may not stay in tune very well. Playing the song in standard tuning may not sound exactly like the recording—you'll miss that menacing depth and growl—but it is a perfectly acceptable alternative. On the road, Joe plays the song in C (down a major 3rd) on his custom built Ernie Ball/Music Man double neck, which features a longer scale baritone neck on top and a standard 6-string neck on the bottom.

Intro/Chorus Riff

This meat-and-potatoes pentatonic riff serves as the powerful backbone of the song. It's very easy to play, with the only real technical considerations being the G5 and A5 chords that are played with the thumb; you get to the roots on the low E string by hooking over the top of the neck. The tips of the ring and index fingers should be used to gently mute the unused open A and G strings, respectively, in each of these chords.

Tune down 2 1/2 steps:
(low to high) B-E-A-D-F♯-B

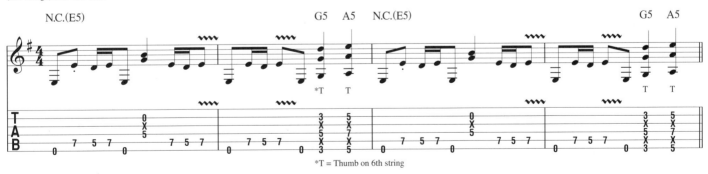

*T = Thumb on 6th string

Verse Riff

This low-key part, played on Dobro, can be a bit challenging to pull off, especially on a standard acoustic or electric guitar. Joe wears a slide on his ring finger for this riff, using it for both the 9th-fret notes and the slides up the D and G strings. The 8th-fret B-string notes are played with the index finger fretting normally, *behind* the slide, a tricky maneuver that's somewhat easier to accomplish on a Dobro, which generally has much higher action than a conventional guitar. Try tilting the slide slightly so it doesn't cover the B string, or lay it across the strings just high enough to clear the string entirely. A little experimentation should lead you to the technique that works best for you. Of course, the best solution is to play it on an actual Dobro, if you have one.

 (Slow demo, 0:19)

TRACK 88

Tune down 2 1/2 steps:
(low to high) B-E-A-D-F♯-B

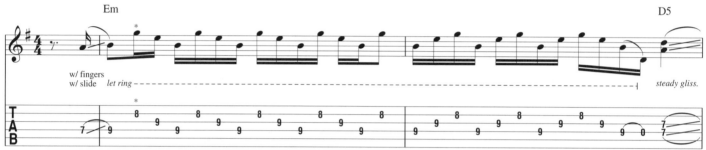

*For next 4 meas., all notes on 2nd string are fretted behind the slide w/ index finger. (Slide worn on ring finger.)

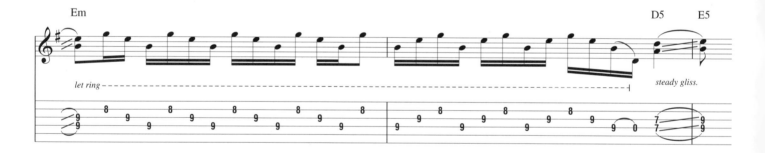

Solo Excerpt # 1

Joe originally planned to play a conventional solo on John Henry but decided to use slide at the last minute, inspired simply by spotting one sitting on a music stand as the band began to record. The resulting improvisation is full of startling sounds and soulful phrases, a wild-yet-restrained outing in comparison with his often blazingly fast solos played with a pick (he uses his fingers here) and no slide. This excerpt, from the beginning of the solo, begins with a bluesy lick centered around the 12th fret, followed by a rising and falling line on the high E string that adds the 9th (F♯) to the E minor pentatonic sound. Apply vibrato only as indicated and keep it under control, using your left-hand index finger to dampen the strings. Joe uses his picking hand thumb to mute the unused strings during the high-E-string line as well.

(Slow demo, 0:12)

TRACK 89

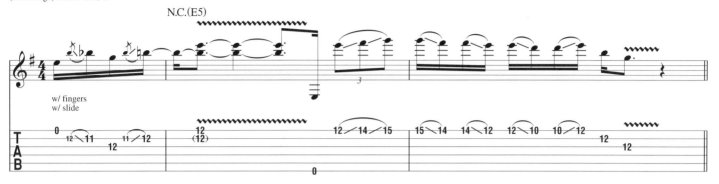

Solo Excerpt #2

The next excerpt begins with a series of long slides down the high E string. Accuracy is paramount on phrases like this. Fall short of your mark or shoot past it, and you'll wind up with a whiny, out-of-tune lick that, at best, is a pale imitation of what Joe does. Don't be content to skate along the neck either; really hit the indicated pitches and make them distinct, with no sliding in between notes except where specifically indicated in the notation. Note the inclusion of the major 6th, C♯, in the latter measures, implying the E Dorian mode (E-F♯-G-A-B-C♯-D).

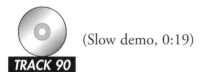

(Slow demo, 0:19)

TRACK 90

Solo Excerpt #3

Our final example finds Joe shifting the mode once again, this time to the somewhat exotic-sounding E Mixolydian (E-F♯-G♯-A-B-C♯-D) in measure 2. The change is short-lived, however. By the end of the measure, he is squarely back in the E blues scale, finishing out the excerpt with lowdown phrases that include the minor 3rd (G) and flatted 5th (B♭). Joe lifts the slide away from the neck during the low-E-string lick in measures 3 and 4, using his index finger for the notes on the 3rd and 5th frets, and his middle finger to play the 6th-fret B♭. If you don't have the 24th fret required to play the last note in the example—and in this book—try laying the slide across the high E string just past the end of the neck; that double high E is up there somewhere!

 (Slow demo, 0:19)

Tune down 2 1/2 steps:
(low to high) B-E-A-D-F♯-B

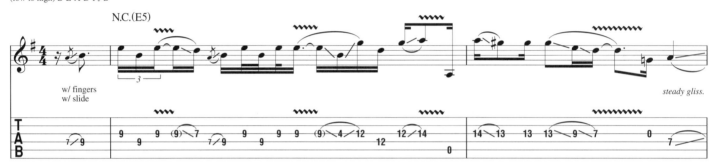

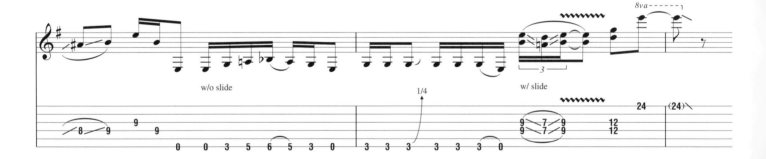

In Conclusion

I sincerely hope you learned something new and exciting in these pages. It would be a great surprise to me if even the most seasoned player couldn't find something here that would stretch his or her abilities, conception, or ears. And, if you take nothing else away from this book, take this, from Joe, on work ethic and giving an honest effort *every time* you pick up the instrument: "At the end of the day, I'm never satisfied with…how I play. You just try to give your best every day, and you give what you have…people will respond to that." The man is humble, a hard worker, and a genuine, down-to-earth guitar hero. He doesn't rest on laurels and accolades. Chances are he's either playing a show, on his way to a show, or practicing his butt off at the very moment you are reading this. What's on your agenda today?

GUITAR NOTATION LEGEND

Guitar music can be notated three different ways: on a *musical staff*, in *tablature*, and in *rhythm slashes*.

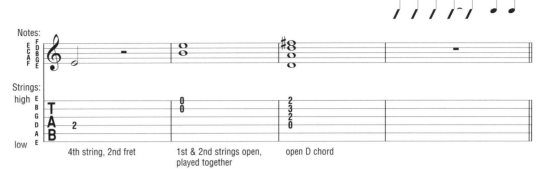

RHYTHM SLASHES are written above the staff. Strum chords in the rhythm indicated. Use the chord diagrams found at the top of the first page of the transcription for the appropriate chord voicings. Round noteheads indicate single notes.

THE MUSICAL STAFF shows pitches and rhythms and is divided by bar lines into measures. Pitches are named after the first seven letters of the alphabet.

TABLATURE graphically represents the guitar fingerboard. Each horizontal line represents a string, and each number represents a fret.

HALF-STEP BEND: Strike the note and bend up 1/2 step.

WHOLE-STEP BEND: Strike the note and bend up one step.

GRACE NOTE BEND: Strike the note and immediately bend up as indicated.

SLIGHT (MICROTONE) BEND: Strike the note and bend up 1/4 step.

BEND AND RELEASE: Strike the note and bend up as indicated, then release back to the original note. Only the first note is struck.

PRE-BEND: Bend the note as indicated, then strike it.

VIBRATO: The string is vibrated by rapidly bending and releasing the note with the fretting hand.

WIDE VIBRATO: The pitch is varied to a greater degree by vibrating with the fretting hand.

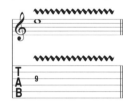

HAMMER-ON: Strike the first (lower) note with one finger, then sound the higher note (on the same string) with another finger by fretting it without picking.

PULL-OFF: Place both fingers on the notes to be sounded. Strike the first note and without picking, pull the finger off to sound the second (lower) note.

LEGATO SLIDE: Strike the first note and then slide the same fret-hand finger up or down to the second note. The second note is not struck.

SHIFT SLIDE: Same as legato slide, except the second note is struck.

TRILL: Very rapidly alternate between the notes indicated by continuously hammering on and pulling off.

TAPPING: Hammer ("tap") the fret indicated with the pick-hand index or middle finger and pull off to the note fretted by the fret hand.

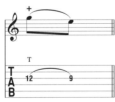

NATURAL HARMONIC: Strike the note while the fret-hand lightly touches the string directly over the fret indicated.

PINCH HARMONIC: The note is fretted normally and a harmonic is produced by adding the edge of the thumb or the tip of the index finger of the pick hand to the normal pick attack.

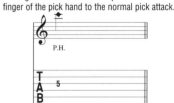

PICK SCRAPE: The edge of the pick is rubbed down (or up) the string, producing a scratchy sound.

MUFFLED STRINGS: A percussive sound is produced by laying the fret hand across the string(s) without depressing, and striking them with the pick hand.

PALM MUTING: The note is partially muted by the pick hand lightly touching the string(s) just before the bridge.

RAKE: Drag the pick across the strings indicated with a single motion.

TREMOLO PICKING: The note is picked as rapidly and continuously as possible.

VIBRATO BAR DIVE AND RETURN: The pitch of the note or chord is dropped a specified number of steps (in rhythm), then returned to the original pitch.

VIBRATO BAR SCOOP: Depress the bar just before striking the note, then quickly release the bar.

VIBRATO BAR DIP: Strike the note and then immediately drop a specified number of steps, then release back to the original pitch.

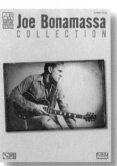
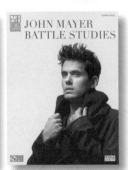